Managing forests as common property

FAO FORESTRY PAPER

136

by
J.E.M. Arnold

2005
Published by Arrangement with the
Food and Agriculture Organization
of the United Nations
by
DAYA PUBLISHING HOUSE
Delhi - 110 035
for Sale and Distribution only in South-East Asia

OVERSEAS
DEVELOPMENT
INSTITUTE

Food
and
Agriculture
Organization
of
the
United
Nations

Rome, 1998

"This book was originally published by the Food and Agriculture Organization of the United Nations (FAO) as FAO Forestry Paper No. 136."

First Indian Edition 2005

ISBN 81-7035-407-2

Published by : **Daya Publishing House**
1123/74, Deva Ram Park
Tri Nagar, Delhi - 110 035
Phone: 27383999
Fax: (011) 23244987
e-mail : dayabooks@vsnl.com
website : www.dayabooks.com

Showroom : 4762-63/23, Ansari Road, Darya Ganj,
New Delhi - 110 002
Phone: 23245578, 23244987

Printed at : **Chawla Offset Printers**
Delhi - 110 052

PRINTED IN INDIA

Foreword

To achieve sustainable development, it is important to understand the impact that different forest management systems, such as communal, private or state, have on both the welfare of local communities and the utilization and conservation of forest resources.

Common property systems have historically governed the management of substantial parts of the world's forest resources. To prevent their overuse, these resources were often subject to some form of effective local control. Now, nearly everywhere, both the resources and the common property systems are facing increasing pressures as populations grow and the economic and political environment changes.

In some cases common property systems have been legislated out of existence, and in other cases local management mechanisms have weakened or disappeared gradually as communities have evolved and changed. Nevertheless, communal management has remained an important option for a great number of communities, and continues to be a potential strategy for the conservation and sustainable use of large parts of the world's forests.

The challenge is to enable both local people and the nation to obtain goods and services that improve livelihoods, without compromising long-term resource and development goals. The need to confront this challenge has taken on a new urgency due to the surge of interest in decentralization. At the same time, changes in ownership and control systems are being considered for vast areas of forest, and new forms of joint management are emerging. Understanding the opportunities and constraints of common property management systems has therefore become both crucial and urgent.

In order to have a greater understanding of the possibilities offered by various tenure and management arrangements for forest lands, a group of researchers was brought together by FAO in the early 1990s to analyse the available literature from Asia, Africa and Latin America on communal forest management. It became clear that these management systems entailed intricate relationships between village groups and local institutions, between individuals and laws that govern the forest, and between governments and villagers. An annotated bibliography emerged from this effort in 1993. The advisory group and FAO then agreed that it was timely to produce a state of knowledge paper on this issue, and requested J.E.M. Arnold to take on this assignment.

J.E.M. Arnold is a well-known authority on managing forests as common property. In this document, he has clarified definitions and analysed indigenous systems and those more recently introduced through projects or development programmes. He has highlighted issues to consider when evaluating the potential for successful communal management. He explores *broad factors* such as policies, population pressures and a suitable economic environment, *local factors* of organizational capacity and motivation to manage in relation to the available resource and *institutional factors* at the government and donor level. He also points out which types of experiences and data are necessary to collect and analyse so that the questions left unanswered may be more effectively addressed. FAO hopes that this study will be a seminal document, which will serve as an important benchmark for future work in the field.

This study is part of a series of documents on forest and tree management. Related documents concerned with tenure, institutional and legal analysis and communal management are discussed in the box on page xi.

Support and funding for *Managing forests as common property* was provided by the multidonor Forests, Trees and People Programme (FTPP), which works to increase livelihoods of women and men through local, sustainable management of tree and forest resources.

Acknowledgements

Many people have contributed to the preparation of this study. In addition, it has benefited from other work on the subject at the Overseas Development Institute and from an earlier review for FAO carried out at the Oxford Forestry Institute. Thanks are due to John Bruce, Mary Hobley, Margaret McKean, Elinor Ostrom and Michael Richards, for making available work in progress and other material, and for helpful advice about the study. The author is also most grateful to Mary Hobley, Marilyn Hoskins, Jonathan Lindsay, Marc de Montalembert and members of the FAO advisory group on common property for reading and commenting on a draft of the publication.

Table of contents

BOXES

ACRONYMS

CAMPFIRE Communal Areas Management Programme for Indigenous Resources
CFSA Communal Forest Stewardship Agreements
CPR Common Pool Resource
DENR Department for the Environment and Natural Resources
FAU County-level forestry associations
FPC Forest Protection Committee
JFM Joint Forest Management
HRMS Hill Resource Management Society
ISF Integrated Social Forestry
NFFAU National Federation of Forestry Associations
PPF Plan Piloto Forestal
RFD Royal Forest Department
SPFEQR Sociedad de Productores Forestales Ejidales de Quintana Roo AC
STK Temporary land use rights certificates
VFA Village Forestry Associations
VPC Village Protection Committee

Other documents related to tree and forest management

The Community Forestry Unit (CFU) and FTPP have developed a series of documents supporting the understanding of local tree and forest management and focusing on three aspects: tenure; institutional and legal analysis; and communal management. These materials address a range of issues related to communal management of tree and forest resources. It is intended that these documents will be relevant to policy-makers as well as practitioners in forestry programmes. The entire set of documents will be useful to universities and training centres.

Tenure

A concept paper examines and clarifies the issues of tenure related to community forestry (Community Forestry Note 5, *Community forestry: rapid appraisal of tree and land tenure*, 1989). A field manual presents rapid appraisal tools for field use Community Forestry Field Manual 4, *Tree and land tenure: rapid appraisal tools*, 1994). A case study from Nepal adapts and illustrates the use of the methodology to obtain tenure information useful for project management (Community Forestry Case Study 9, *Tree and land tenure in the Eastern Terai, Nepal. A case study from the Siraha and Saptari Districts, Nepal*, 1993). A case study from Madagascar illustrates the use of the field manual in policy level analysis (Community Forestry Case Study 10, *Tree and land tenure: using rapid appraisal to study natural resource management. A case study from Anivorano, Madagascar*, 1995).

Institutional and Legal Analysis

A concept paper analyses elements for understanding rules followed by stake holding groups related to attributes of the tree resource and to incentives or disincentives for community members to expand or to manage tree and woodland resources (Community Forestry Note 10, *A framework for analyzing institutional incentives in community forestry*, 1992). A field manual applies these concepts to field conditions for increasing successful planning, implementation and evaluation of forestry activities (Community Forestry Field Manual 7, *Crafting institutional arrangements for community forestry*, 1997). A working paper is being developed which analyses the legal environments in which local forest management takes place and in what ways these often vulnerable systems can be supported through laws and regulations (to be published in 1998).

Communal Management

This group of publications starts with an analysis of relevant literature from Latin America, Asia and Sahelien Africa (Community Forestry Note 11, *Common forest resource management: annotated bibliography of Asia, Africa and Latin America*, 1993). This publication raised issues confirming that literature from the various sites in different or even the same regions was not comparable as consistent data had not been collected from site to site. FAO initiated development of a data collection list and a relational data base for organizing and analysing data, the International Forestry Resources and Institutions (IFRI) Programme, developed at Indiana University with the collaboration of a number of institutions and with an international network of research centres and researchers. This programme will publish a working paper about the information developed through IFRI.

Chapter 1. Background

Introduction

Historically, substantial parts of the forest resources in many regions of the world have been managed as common property. In a wide range of situations, people have depended on the outputs of forest resources that were best controlled and managed collectively. This was often because forests and woodland formed part of larger systems in which land needed to be controlled by the users as a group, or because rural households needed to fill gaps in the material and income flows from their own resources by drawing on nearby areas of forest, woodland or scrubland.

In the past, such forest resources were often subject to some form of local control by those who used them, in order to prevent their overuse. Now, both the resource and the management and use system are nearly everywhere facing increasing pressures from growing populations and the effects of economic and political changes. Nevertheless, land use practices that incorporate periods of forest or bush fallow, or that require access to off-farm forest or woodland resources, continue to be critical to the functioning of many rural economic systems. Collective management therefore remains an important option. Local control is also very relevant to current moves to reduce the size and cost of government by decentralizing and devolving responsibilities and activities, and by achieving a greater degree of involvement and participation by local stakeholders.

The purpose of this study is to bring together available information about the role of common property as a system of governance and its present relevance to forest management and use, to review the historical record of common property systems that have disappeared or survived, to examine the experience of selected contemporary collective management programmes in different countries, and to identify the main factors that appear to determine success or failure at the present time. The final chapter of the study summarizes implications for policy, research and practice.

Defining Common Property Concepts and Terms[1]

Common Property or Open Access?

Discussion of common property management needs to start with an understanding of basic terms and concepts, because "the term 'common property' has been largely misunderstood and falsely interpreted for the past two to three decades" (Bromley and Cernea, 1989).

Over the years, 'common property' has all too often been used to refer both to land or resources available to all and consequently not owned or managed by anyone, and also to situations where access is limited to a specific group that holds rights in common. The confusion between the two has been aggravated by the way a 1968 article by Garrett Hardin on the 'tragedy of the commons' has been interpreted and understood. In this article Hardin set out a parable intended to explain overgrazing in a hypothetical medieval English commons. Each herdsman has the incentive to increase the number of animals he grazes in order to maximize his individual returns. As the commons resource is finite, doing so will in due course deplete and destroy it. In the meantime

[1] This section draws in particular on McKean and Ostrom, 1995, and on related works by these two authors (McKean, 1995; Ostrom, 1990 and 1994).

the gain to each herdsman from adding to his herd more than offsets his share of the loss due to the damage done to the commons. Since all the herdsmen adopt the same individual logic, in the end they all lose. Hardin compared this inevitable result to a classical Greek tragedy, in which those involved know that the disaster is coming but are unable to do anything about it.

Though this is not explicit in the article, the situation that Hardin was describing was in practice one that is more accurately termed 'unregulated open access' use. However, it was widely interpreted as applying to any situation involving use of a resource used in common by several or many users. Failure to recognize 'common property' as a regulated form of resource tenure and use, managed by a group of users with exclusive rights to do so, and the consequent presumption that such use is destined inevitably to lead to degradation of the resource, has had a profound impact on thinking, policy and practice related to control and management of forests and other natural resources. In particular, it has contributed powerfully to the pursuit of land distribution policies that favour individual private landholdings, and has helped to justify state control of forest resources, ostensibly to ensure protection and productive use.

There is also confusion because 'common property' is used to refer to a resource, or to the collective system for managing the resource, or to both. In this study, therefore, the term 'common pool resource' (CPR) will be used to characterize the resource, and the term 'common property' (or 'common property regime') will be reserved for situations in which the resource is managed as common property (McKean and Ostrom, 1995).

Institutional Factors

In order to regulate the use and management of a common pool forest resource, there must be institutions that authorize and secure use by a particular group of users (to the exclusion of others), and institutions that set rules to govern this use and monitor and enforce those rules. Thus, common property systems can function only if the group is organized, or can organize itself, to set and implement such rules, provide individual members with inputs and services that are more effective when organized collectively, and provide a mechanism for negotiation and liaison with the state and other external entities.

It is also necessary to ensure that the user group is empowered to exercise the exclusive use rights that it claims. Much misunderstanding and confusion has arisen in this respect because of failure to distinguish between the rights to use a resource and the rights related to the resource itself. Rights may exist or be established that enable persons, or groups of persons, other than the owner to use the resource or some specified output of that resource.[2] This becomes particularly important in understanding uses in forests where much of the resource is owned by the state, but most usage is by individual, collective or industrial entities, frequently with multiple users exercising rights to different products or to use at different times of the year.

The distinction between stock (the forest) and flow (output) is another aspect of forest resource management that is often overlooked or misunderstood. The institutional arrangements for producing and selling forest products (flow units) are quite likely to be different from those controlling and managing the forest stock (the resource). Problems and issues can arise separately in each, and the governance arrangements it takes to handle both successfully are frequently complex (McKean and Ostrom, 1995).

Perhaps the most important area of misunderstanding relates to the relative merits of private and common property.[3] The preference for private property that underlies so much of the transfer out of common property rests on the argument that well-defined property rights are needed in order to ensure that the holder will use the resource efficiently and responsibly, and that only

---

[2] Equally, systems based on communal ownership or control of the land may contain tenurial niches in which individual and family property also exists. Common property should therefore not be confused with 'communal tenure' (Bruce, 1998).

[3] The literature on property generally recognizes four categories: public, private, common property and open access. These categories are usually distinguished on the basis of (a) the ease with which potential users can be excluded from access to the good ('excludability'), and (b) whether using a portion of the good shrinks the supply that remains ('subtractibility'). 'Public' goods, which are non-excludable and non-subtractible (e.g. street lights, clean air) contrast with private goods, which are both excludable and subtractible. Common property goods lie somewhere in between the two, and share some of the characteristics of each; exclusion is difficult, and they are subtractible (Bromley and Cernea, 1989; NAS, 1986; Ostrom, 1990).

private property rights provide this security. However, much of the debate about privatization assumes that private property is synonymous with individual ownership. This overlooks the fact that the definition of private property actually has to do with rights, not who holds them, and that much private property is held by business partnerships and shareholder-owned industrial corporations, and other collective entities.

Thus, private property and common property can be seen not as mutually exclusive, but as two types of property with a good deal in common (Bruce, 1998). As access to use of common property is confined to members of a defined user group, which excludes other potential beneficiaries, the common property therefore has some of the attributes of shared private property. Put another way, common property is a way of privatizing the rights to use a resource without having to divide the resource into individual holdings (McKean, 1995).

It is therefore argued that: "Like individual parcellation, common property gives resource owners the incentive to husband their resources, to make investments in resource quality and to manage them sustainably and thus efficiently over the long term" (McKean, 1995). However, as has already been noted, common property rights to forests often apply only to use of products and not to, or in lesser measure to, the resource. Where rights to change the use of a resource, or to sell or otherwise alienate it, rest with others (e.g. the state or a private landowner), the argument that common property rights are as strong as private ownership has more limited force.

Circumstances Favouring Common Property

The principal argument in support of privatization to individuals[4] or expropriation by the state is based on the assumption that the cohesion and discipline necessary for effective collective management cannot be achieved or will break down, resulting in unregulated open access overuse with a 'tragedy of the commons' conclusion. Implicit in this argument is the assumption that circumstances no longer permit effective collective control or, more fundamentally, that the changing environment within which individuals must operate fosters behaviour patterns inimical to collective cooperation.

However, these arguments fail to take into account those factors which encourage collective action, and the self-regulating capabilities of groups of users (Runge, 1986). These arguments also overlook reasons why the alternatives to common property management may themselves not be sustainable. The same reasons that make it difficult to secure exclusion from a CPR may make it even more difficult to achieve the degree of separation, exclusion and protection necessary to privatize it. Individual private use can also lead to overuse and degradation, particularly on the low-productivity sites characteristic of many common property areas. Equally, the state may not be able to control, manage or prevent degradation to a resource it has expropriated (Berkes *et al.*, 1989).

Furthermore, privatization is unlikely to improve the efficiency of meeting the needs of those who used the resource as common property. In fact, by transferring control of the resource to a limited number of individuals who thereby acquire the social and legal sanction to exclude others, privatization is likely to exacerbate the problems of those without access to private property (Bromley and Cernea, 1989).

The thrust toward expropriation or privatization also tends to ignore the fact that breakdowns in common property systems may reflect deficiencies in policy or policy implementation, rather than their appropriateness for managing a resource. For example, common property seldom has the same degree of support in law, or elicits the same response from the authorities when threatened, as private property (Bromley and Cernea, 1989; Bruce, 1998).

The central question that needs to be addressed is: Under what circumstances does common property provide the best match between the resource and the economic, social and institutional context within which it is located? As long as resources are abundant, and pressures on them are low, the need for regulation and rules is unlikely to arise, and open access use is likely to be as appropriate as any other regime.

[4] In the rest of this document, the term 'privatization' is used in this sense of allocation of ownership or exclusive rights of use to individuals.

Box 1: Advantages of Common Property Regimes[1]

Indivisibility: The resource may have physical traits that preclude parcelling; the production system may not be amenable to division or demarcation. It may not be possible to establish boundaries around the resource system, or the resources may be mobile over a large territory. Forests may seem more divisible (and fenceable) than other kinds of resource systems, but in fact, where forests are being managed not only for products that can be taken from them but also for their value in protecting water and soil, not to mention local climate, forests need to be managed in very large units.

Uncertainty in location of productive zones: In fragile environments nature may impose great uncertainty on the productivity of any particular section of a resource system, and the location of the unproductive sections cannot easily be predicted from year to year, but the 'average' or 'total' productivity of the entire area may be fairly steady over the years. In this situation, the resource system is stationary and may even have fairly obvious boundaries, but its productive portions are not stationary. In such systems resource users may well prefer to share the entire area and decide together where to concentrate use at a particular time, rather than parcelling the area into individual tracts and thereby imposing the risk of total disaster on those users whose parcels turn out to be unproductive ones in a given year.

Productive efficiency via internalizing externalities: In many resource systems, uses in one zone immediately affect uses and productivity in another: deforesting a hillside ruins the water supply and downhill soil quality. If different people own the uphill forests and the downhill fields, and if they make their decisions independently and separately, they may well cause harm to one another. If these externalities are substantial, creating a common property regime to make resource management decisions jointly can provide a mechanism for acknowledging and internalizing the multiple negative externalities that are implicit in resource use in this setting. People who use a common property regime to manage their uphill forests all share ownership of the upland forests, restrain timbering to prevent soil erosion and damage to fields below, and earn more from their downhill farms than they sacrifice by not cutting as much uphill timber.

Administrative efficiency: Even if resources are readily divisible into parcels, and where intensive independent use of adjacent parcels does not produce problematic externalities, the administrative support to enforce property rights to individual parcels may not be available. The society may be too poor to support a large court system to enforce individual land titles, and even low-cost fencing would be expensive by this society's standards. Creating a common property regime here is a way of substituting collective management rules, which function as imaginary fences and informal courts internal to the user group, for what is missing. It is less expensive in these circumstances, and it is within the power of a group of resource users to create.

[1] In many situations more than one of these conditions applies, particularly where people are interested in making good use of a resource system capable of generating multiple products.

Source: McKean, 1995

Historically, common property regimes have evolved where the demand on a resource has become too great to tolerate open access use any longer, so that property rights in the resource have to be created, and where other factors make it impossible or undesirable to allocate the resource to individuals (McKean, 1995).

A common property regime can also emerge as a way to secure control over a territory or a resource, to exclude outsiders or to regulate the individual use by members of the community. The choice of property regime may also reflect historical feudal and conquest institutions (Bruce, 1998).

Common property, like any other property or governance regime, is likely to be maintained only as long as it is appropriate to the changing situation in which it is found. Change may be towards individual or state management, or back to open access, or, as is found in many forest situations, towards some combination of rights and regimes (Berkes *et al.*, 1989; Bromley and Cernea, 1989; Bruce, 1998). However, resources can continue to be managed as common property for long periods in the midst of fundamental economic and social changes when this is the most appropriate form of management. For instance, it is still an active system of forest management in parts of Europe.

Forest Resources and Outputs as Common Property

Box 1 (McKean, 1995) identifies a number of types of natural resource situations in which placing property rights with groups can be more efficient than trying to allocate the rights, or the resource, to individuals. The potential advantages of collective control of forest resources can be summarized as follows:

- Some resources are simply indivisible or, like many forest ecosystems, have to be managed in their entirety in order to maintain the interactive environment needed to produce some of their outputs (including mobile resources such as wildlife).
- In some large resource systems, such as range and woodland in arid areas, the location of the most productive zones can vary from year to year.
- In resource systems subjected to heavy population pressure or with congested and competing uses, coordination among users is essential to cope with problems caused by multiple uses or with interrelationships such as the effect on farmers of forest use in upland areas in a watershed and land use in lower areas.
- Group control, and thus group enforcement of rules, can be an efficient way of coping with the costs of monitoring otherwise porous boundaries and of enforcing restraints on use within those boundaries.

Forest resources that exhibit some or all of these characteristics are likely to be good candidates for management as common property regimes. However, even where this is so, users of forest products often have the option of obtaining supplies from sources other than the forest. For example, fuel may be obtained from trees managed by households on their farmlands, or it may be purchased. Therefore, the decision to manage a forest or woodland resource as common property may be less clear-cut than it is for resources such as irrigation water or many fish stocks, where there is no effective alternative that would ensure sustainable supplies.

In addition, forest-use situations are often complex, involving multiple products as well as multiple user groups that have different ethnic, geographic or economic profiles and different interests and priorities. This, of course, increases the potential for dispute and conflict, which increases the difficulty and cost of developing and maintaining effective institutions to monitor and control use.

Given this diversity and variation from situation to situation and over time, there can be no widely applicable or universal models. Analysis needs to be pursued within a framework that recognizes this diversity. Discussion in the literature on common property, and on its relevance to forest management, suggests a number of factors that could be important in this respect:

- the existence of a suitable resource;
- the role of forest products in livelihood and land use systems;
- social and cultural cohesion and authority at the user group level;
- the impact of economic and demographic change on user populations; and
- the impact of policies and legislation on their institutional environment.

The examination and analysis that follow in this study will focus on these factors.

Chapter 2. Learning from systems with historical and indigenous origins

In this chapter we look at systems of management of forests as common property that have been important in the past and at their evolution. The focus is on identifying factors that appear to account for their decline or breakdown, where this has happened, and for the survival of those that are still functioning, and for the emergence of new indigenous systems in the recent past. Particular attention is paid to the circumstances in which common property systems have emerged or remain in existence in response to indigenous initiatives and factors. The term 'indigenous' is used here to differentiate systems with local-level origins from systems initiated, or heavily influenced, by interventions from governments or other outsiders. These systems and programmes will be discussed in the next chapter.

Ideally, such a review would be organized according to the main themes that we expect to be important in explaining the history of common property as a system of forest management, i.e. those outlined in the closing paragraph of the previous chapter. In this case the available material is predominantly organized geographically, because most of it is derived from case studies and any synthesizing has been done by country or region rather than by theme. However, comparisons of this kind can have the value of assembling and assessing the experience of numbers of situations that do share some elements of commonality of ecological conditions, and possibly of ethnic and socio-economic background as well.

This chapter first examines the findings of studies and reviews relating to the geographical regions where common property systems of forest management have been most important. It then attempts to develop from this information an assessment of factors that seem to be common, first, to histories of decline, and, second, to systems that are still in existence.

Southeast Asia

Though this large region encompasses many different situations, much communal management of forest and forest land historically developed around swidden agriculture in order to control use of land or soil, and around rights to use of natural vegetation that was subject to group control. Village or clan households typically had the right to cultivate specific plots and to claim exclusive collection rights from useful tree species. People from outside had to ask permission and sometimes pay rent or a fee for collection rights. In many cases, the institutional coordination of land use practices of swidden cultivators was relatively weak, based on public discussion and without strong community sanctions. The strongest group action often was directed at preventing outsiders from monopolizing specific resources (Mol and Wiersum, 1993).

Many of these traditional management systems have weakened and broken down as colonial regimes and national governments have progressively introduced legislation to restrict local land rights to lands actually being cultivated, and as the introduction of new land use practices involving commercial cropping lessened local interest in forest products (Poffenberger, 1990). Communal ownership and management of swidden areas have consequently diminished. In many areas, land (including fallow) is now typically owned by individual households and worked by individual household labour forces or reciprocal, but not communal, work groups (Dove, 1983).

During recent decades there has been a huge expansion in the areas designated as state forests in some of the main countries of the region. Reasons for this include government interests in tapping valuable forest resources, increasing pressures to exercise physical control over upland areas for strategic reasons or because of their importance as a land bank for surplus lowland populations, and growing concerns about preventing downstream damage resulting from overuse of upland areas. As the extent of state control has increased, its focus has tended to shift from control over population, labour or particular species to territorial control. Though agrarian legislation in support of development of rural populations usually exists, it often has been overridden by forestry legislation that severely restricts local people's activities in areas designated as forests (Lynch and Talbott, 1995; Peluso *et al.*, 1995).

Although the combination of government restrictions, logging activities and other commercial enterprises, and impacts of demographic and local economic changes have generally combined to discourage and undermine local forest management, some common property systems have survived, and in some situations new ones have emerged. This is particularly the case in hill areas, which have only come under pressure relatively recently, but common property systems also can be found in the remaining forested areas in the more intensively settled lowlands.

For example, in north and northeast Thailand, the most resilient forms of common property usually have been traditional sacred forest protection systems. In addition, some communities protect watershed forests and areas of communal woodland set aside for fuel and other needs. Many of these local forest regimes began to emerge about 30 years ago in response to growing shortages of water and forest products. Increasing local protection and management also reflect a more intensive utilization of their resources by communities, in response to growing pressures from the state, loggers and other outsiders.

Increasingly, communities are concerned with giving more formal institutional form to their forest protection initiatives, e.g. by having them endorsed by village councils, recording them as written rules and organizing patrols to monitor adherence to the rules. At present, such communal forest areas have no legal basis because forest land is considered state property, though it is widely exploited by commercial users and settlers on a *de facto* open access basis. Legislation is being drafted, but the government's priority is to regularize the position of squatters on alienable forest land by granting them individual rights, though this focus could undermine collective management. A draft Community Forest Act will give more tenurial security, but is designed more to support new programmes than to empower existing indigenous group systems, and would not cover common property systems in the conservation areas where many of the indigenous regimes are located (Anan Ganjanapan, 1995).

Sometimes forest departments are willing and able to mitigate the impacts of legislation vesting control of forest areas in the central state by working out arrangements with local people that enable the latter to maintain at least a measure of control over management of a local forest resource. Examples of this have been reported in northern Thailand and parts of Indonesia (Fox, 1996).

Collective control can also be found where it proves to be consistent with modernization of local livelihood systems. In parts of West Kalimantan, Indonesia, for instance, people have adapted their resource use and management practices in response to reduction in the land area to which they have access and to greater exposure to markets as the rural road infrastructure has been extended. A feature of this adaptation has been the incorporation and intensification of cultivation within the forest of tree crops with economic value, such as rubber, rattan and durian. This has been achieved within local control systems that introduce greater individual control over the production and marketing of products, alongside elements of the earlier collective systems for managing the resource (Peluso and Padoch, 1996).

South Asia

The South Asia region also encompasses a wide range of ecological and cultural conditions. Though there are marked differences between hill and plain and between forested and agricultural regions, forest products from CPRs have historically constituted an important part of livelihood systems nearly everywhere. For large numbers of people this is still the case.

Much of the area has a common history of the state exercising progressively greater control over forests. Though earlier rulers frequently claimed control over forest areas, this seldom amounted to more than attempts to collect royalties. It was during the British colonial period that government started to lay legal claim to use of much of the forest estate, and to exercise these new powers. In the postindependence period, with the abolishment of the princely states and the expropriation of their forests, this control by the central government was greatly extended.

The initiatives of the colonial government, from the mid-nineteenth century on, were directed at gaining control over the wealth represented by the forests and consequently focused on commercial forest management. Early legislation limited private property to continuously cultivated land and vested considerable power in the Indian Forest Service. Many local people lost their rights of access to the forests during the process of forest reservation, and those 'rights' that were legally recognized at that time have tended to be progressively circumscribed, downgraded from 'rights' to 'privileges', or extinguished by subsequent legislation and practices. By 1980, nearly 23 percent of India's total land area was under state management, while the rights of an estimated 300 million rural resource users had become increasingly unclear (Lindsay, 1994; Poffenberger and Singh, 1996).

The impact of these changes is best examined by looking separately at common property in the three main agro-ecological zones: the central forest belt, the hills and mountains in the north and west of the subregion, and the low rainfall plains that occupy most of the rest of India.[5]

[5] In addition to the references cited, this discussion draws on Arnold and Stewart, 1991.

Forest Belt In the forest belt across central India, with predominantly tribal populations, CPRs have always been an important source of forest produce for sale, food for lean periods and medicinal plants and other products for local use. Because these forest products also account for major portions of forest department revenues in the respective states, conflicts between state and local claims have been widespread.

Difficulties in defining common rights, and erosion of local rights in the nineteenth century as the state nationalized forest areas, led to a situation in which most of the land became state or private property, irrespective of its actual use. Many areas ended up being officially classified as forest or revenue lands with very limited individual or village rights. In other areas poorer villagers lost control to high-caste groups or to commercial interests.

Nevertheless, it is in the more heavily forested states that indigenous local management systems are presently most numerous and strongest. It has been estimated that in the forest belt across India there are at least 10 000 forest protection groups managing areas in forests designated as Protected Forests, in which state control is less intense and in which there is generally more scope for use by local people than is the case in Reserved Forests. Many of these informal systems, dating from the 1970s, reflect a response to a growing scarcity of forest products, a perceived growth in outside threats, and a growth in activities of local NGOs able to support such initiatives (Poffenberger, 1996).

These forest protection groups are typically very small, often based in a single, ethnically homogeneous hamlet and frequently functioning within broader hamlet-level management activities (see Box 2). Initially, forest protection groups concentrated on control of harvesting and use but, in order to improve productivity, they have become increasingly involved in more active management of their forest areas. Some also have taken on management of areas of Reserved Forest.

Increasingly, groups have been seeking more formal authorization for their activities in order to strengthen their position in dealing with outsiders and the state. The forest department is empowered to authorize locally organized forest protection systems, and many have been authorized.

Box 2: Characteristics of Indigenous Forest Protection Groups in India

Forest/poverty/tribal interface. Forest protection activities appear most common in areas that are characterized by significant concentrations of forest, poverty and high tribal populations. Cultural and economic ties to the forest often lead tribals to play a leadership role in establishing controls over degrading forests, although low-caste and low-income groups are also active.

Forest degradation. In central India, forests that reach a critical stage of degradation are often targeted for protection by communities. There may be a degradation or scarcity threshold at which management actions are likely to occur. There is also recognition that devegetation and topsoil loss will undermine the forest's capacity for recovery.

Local environmental concerns. Forest protection groups are frequently formed with little or no outside intervention but as a result of local concerns over resource depletion and environmental changes. Changing microclimates, falling groundwater levels and disappearing biological diversity are frequently cited by villagers as critical problems. Deteriorating linkages between agriculture and forest ecosystems are also widely acknowledged. Perceived threats from outside forest users are also catalysts for social action.

Local leadership. Local leaders, including elders, teachers and village intellectuals, as well as youth club members, provide guidance to villagers in reaching decisions, formulating strategies and coordinating forest protection with other communities and the forest department. Local leaders often have greater credibility with the community than political representatives from neighbouring hamlets that fall within the same administrative unit, probably because of their greater immediate social accountability.

Cohesive communities. Forest protection is often localized in small residential clusters frequently comprised of a single caste or tribe of 20 to 50 households. Because they exist below the lowest level of local government (*panchayat*), these groups have fewer problems with divisive political factions and appear better able to reach agreements regarding management. Multihamlet forest organizations appear less stable and tend to divide into single-hamlet management units over time.

Internal process. Community forest protection emerges as a process of social change and adaptation to growing environmental problems. The management transition responds to local resources, needs and capacities for implementation. It may be influenced, and the process accelerated, by external policies and projects.

Presence of supportive actors. In many cases, villagers have been encouraged by small NGOs and forestry field staff in their decision to begin forest protection activities. Such actors can be instrumental as an initial catalyst and can also accelerate the emergence of new groups and their consolidation.

Ecological resilience. Both community and joint [community/forest department] forest management appear to work well where natural forests have retained their ecological resilience, allowing a rapid and visible biological regeneration and a corresponding increase in the flow of non-timber forest products.

Source: Poffenberger, 1996

However, in some areas some reluctance has been evident, in part because of concern that the spread of local management could encroach on the position of the forest department (Kant *et al.*, 1991; Poffenberger, 1996).

The spread and growth in numbers of local protection groups in the forest zone has been attributed to the presence of strong informal village organizations, the ambiguous status of Protected Forests (which allows some flexibility and innovation in arrangements with local users), and the benefits to both villagers and the state of bringing degraded forest under management (Kant *et al.*, 1991).

Hill Areas

Forests used as CPRs in hill areas are a main source of the high inputs of green manure required to sustain upland agricultural production, and of grazing and collected fodder for livestock, which play a major role in the agricultural economy. They are also the source of the considerable amounts of wood needed for cooking, heating and house construction. Forest areas per household can be substantial. At lower altitudes, in areas where irrigation permits profitable agriculture, protection of water resources is an important land use issue.

In the hill areas of the Indian Himalayas, Shivaliks and Western Ghats, forest CPRs comprise 60 to 80 percent of the area. There is usually a common interest in how the resource should be used because extensive rights and privileges pertaining to the forests have been codified, and interhousehold patterns of use of forest products tend to be similar. However, the fact that forests are predominantly under the control of forest departments seems to have discouraged communities from investing in local forest management institutions in most areas (an exception being the Van Panchayats of Uttar Pradesh, discussed later in this study).

The isolation and enforced self-sufficiency of hill communities in Nepal have led to a stronger tradition of collective management. By the mid-nineteenth century much use was in practice controlled by local users, even though a large part of the hill forests was nominally held by the state or by those acting on behalf of the state. The end of the Rana rule and the subsequent nationalization of all forests in 1957 (a measure that the state was unable to enforce) seems to have encouraged more local groups to bring the forest areas they used under their own control in order to secure their access to them (Fisher, 1989). In a 1982 survey of a large part of the hill area, it was found that 36 percent of local leaders reported the existence of some form of collective system for protecting an area (or areas) of local public forest. More than half of these collectives had come into existence after the forests were nationalized (Campbell and Bhattarai, 1983). New indigenous local systems continue to be established.

Though the situation varies widely from place to place, such local collective management generally exhibits the following characteristics.

- Forest areas are managed by a group consisting of the households that traditionally use the area for forest produce, which form an entity much smaller than the panchayat, or even the village.
- Villagers' participation appears to be motivated primarily by perceived shortages as forest resources diminish (although strong local leadership can also be important in initiating management systems).
- Management systems have developed in areas where shortages have emerged, but not where they have become too severe to be remedied by managed use of the remaining resource alone.
- Most existing management systems tend to be very conservative, avoiding systems of harvesting that would be difficult to enforce (in general, use of forests is controlled by restricting access to certain times of the year or by rotating access spatially).
- Most user groups discourage breaches of the management rules by employing forest watchers (paid in grain by every household, except the poorest).
- Conflicts between livestock and forest management are the most common problem (the most effective management systems are in areas where animals are largely stall-fed or under year-round supervision).
- Proximity to markets for forest fuel products also tends to undermine forest management, as it is hard to prevent poaching in areas near market centres (Campbell *et al.*, 1987; Fisher, 1989; Messerschmidt, 1987; Molnar, 1981).

Low Rainfall Plains In the dry, rain-fed plains that characterize much of South Asia outside the hill and forest regions, the main role of CPRs has been to complement the highly variable level of private agricultural production. Vegetation on common pool lands around villages helps farmers defend themselves against the risk of unstable rainfall, providing a major source of fodder, food and saleable products during the long period when there is little or no crop production or a lack of stored supplies from the last harvest. This role is especially important during extended periods of drought.

Traditionally, the sustainability of CPRs was protected by an array of controls, mainly designed and enforced at the local level. Historically, uncultivated land was held as a pool for future expansion of cultivation. Marginal lands within villages were often reserved as village commons in order to prevent their use for arable farming and to allow them to be used less intensively for fodder or trees. As pressures on the available arable land have increased, a large percentage of the draught animals needed for dryland agriculture have been supported by grazing and fodder from non-arable CPRs.

A seminal study by Jodha (1986, 1990) of changes in CPR availability, management and use between 1950 and 1980, gives us a fuller picture of what has happened in this area than we have for other areas (see Box 3). Jodha found that the status of common property regimes had been severely weakened by the introduction of land reforms (which led to abolition of a number of levies and taxes on CPR users); the replacement of traditional village leadership with elected vil-

Box 3: Process of Depletion of Common Property Resources in the Dry Regions of India

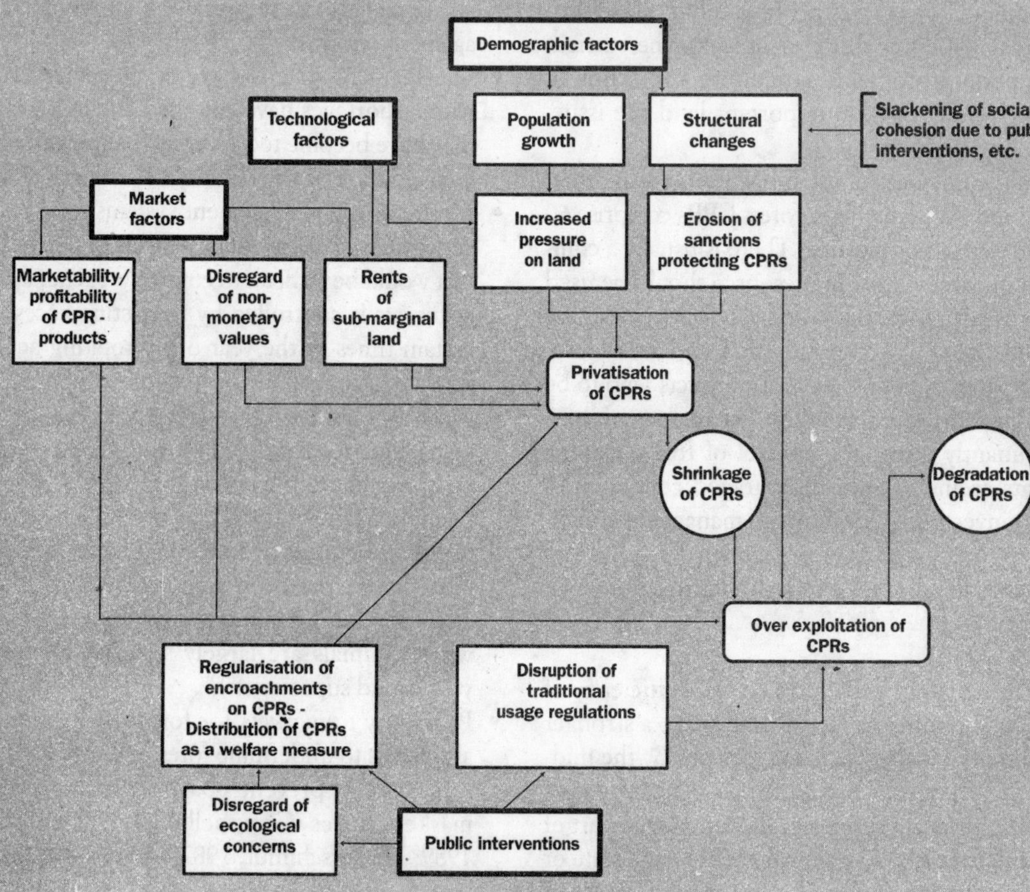

Source: Jodha, 1990

Box 4: Measures Adopted by Different Groups in Response to Decline in Area and Productivity of CPRs, and in Management Systems for CPRs, in Dry Regions of India

Rural rich

1. Withdrawal from common pool resources (CPRs) as user of products (opportunity cost of labour higher than value of products from CPRs)
2. Increased reliance on alternative options:
   - use of on-farm biomass supplies (stall feeding, etc.)
   - use of non-renewable/external resources (e.g. substituting stone fencing for thorn fencing, rubber tires for wooden wheels on carts, iron tools for local wooden ones)
3. Private pressures on CPRs as assets:
   - grabbing common pool lands
   - preventing others from using seasonal CPRs (private croplands during off-season)
4. Approach to CPR management:
   - indifference to decline of CPRs
   - influencing the legal and administrative measures that affect community resources through the local political process

Rural poor

1. Use of CPRs as an important source of sustenance (complementarity of common property and private property activities)
2. Acceptance of inferior options (opportunity cost of labour lower than value of products of degraded CPRs)
3. Measures reflecting desperation:
   - premature harvesting of CPR products
   - removal of roots/base of products
   - overcrowding and overexploitation of CPRs
   - use of hitherto unusable inferior products

Rural community (general)

1. Acceptance of CPRs as open access resources (overexploitation without user obligations or regulations)
2. Selective approach to specific CPR units (despite general neglect of CPRs, concern demonstrated for some units)
3. Focus on other 'uses' of CPRs:
   - in seeking government subsidies and relief
   - in pursuing factional quarrels
   - in supporting populist programmes, etc.
4. Part of non-operating legal and administrative measures
5. Structural changes and focus on alternative sources:
   - changes in livestock composition (e.g. replacing cattle by sheep or goats)
   - agroforestry initiatives (e.g. revival of indigenous agroforestry practices)

Source: adapted from Jodha, 1990

lage councils (which resulted in decreased regulation of common land use); expanded private landownership, expanded credit and subsidies for animals; and more marketing links for CPR-related products (mainly milk, meat, wool, fuel, and other bush and tree products). Only 10 percent of the communities that in 1950 had exercised controls, such as rotational grazing, seasonal restrictions and watchmen, still had those controls in 1980, while use of fines, taxes and fees had ceased altogether.

- The size of communal lands has been greatly reduced because of the large-scale redistribution of land to individuals under land reform programmes, and because of encroachment. The remaining area is typically heavily degraded and under open access usage, and the range, quality and quantity of products collected have often been sharply reduced. Nevertheless, the rural poor are still heavily dependent on CPRs. In his study villages, Jodha found that from 84 to 100 percent of poor households depended on CPRs for fuel, fodder and food items (compared with no more than 20 percent of richer households). Poor households also obtained from 14 to 23 percent of their income from products harvested from CPRs (Jodha, 1990).

Richer farmers have been able to hold on to submarginal lands but keep most of it under private fallow. As the demand for fodder increases and the common pool lands shrink, there has been an increasing tendency to privatize the crop by-products which provide seasonal CPRs. The relative importance of CPRs in dryland areas thus varies significantly among households, with the poor being much more dependent on them and the rich more interested in privatization. This increasing differentiation within villages has been accompanied by increasing conflicts about how CPRs should be used (see Box 4).

Some local management systems have survived, at least in part. Basing his study on an analysis of 176 specific common pool resources for which there was evidence of at least one instance of local interest in protecting the CPR, Jodha (1990) found that small size, isolation and maintenance of traditional social sanctions are village-level factors associated with preservation of common property management. More specifically, greater distance from market centres, smaller and more visible CPRs, less occupational change, less factionalism, less socio-economic differentiation and less dependence on state patronage were found to be important.

In addition, common property management appeared to be related to a number of other factors (Jodha, 1990).

- Most instances of common property management were by-products of other developments, such as factional quarrels in the villages, specific conditions of government grants to the villages and adherence to certain rituals and religious sanctions.
- Higher CPR productivity and yield induced better management, particularly where the gains were shared more equally.
- Location, size and proximity to the village played positive roles in management of CPRs.
- Genuine concern about degradation and misuse of CPRs could induce local action.

Sub-Saharan Africa

Traditionally, management of sub-Saharan forests has been linked to land and the use of land for agricultural and pastoral purposes, with large areas under extensively managed fallow at any one time. Forests, woodland and trees have been important sources of food, fodder and grazing, fuel, construction materials and, more recently, income. Where fallow and active uses alternate, selected areas of woodland or forest were often set aside, notably as sacred groves. Within communally managed forest resources, there usually are different tenure arrangements for different areas of forest and different rules for different products within the forest.

Historically, the institutions that governed the allocation and use of land also governed the use and management of forests. Rights to use of land stemmed from lineage in pastoral areas and from descent and residence in areas of crop agriculture. Rights to cultivation and tree harvesting may be held separately from those connected with land; rights to use of forest products, as well as to use of land, are often associated with investment of labour (Fortmann, 1984; Shepherd, 1992).

Within this general framework of natural resource tenure and use there has been wide variation from system to system, and between different situations. Over time many came to exhibit a hierarchy of tenure relations reflecting systems imposed by conquest, or simply as a result of the migrations that moved populations of different origins into others' territories throughout history. Customary tenure also usually reflected variations in the situation and practice from community to community (Mortimore, 1996).

A feature of these indigenous systems was their continuous adjustment to such changes. The extent of the change brought about by colonial administrations varied considerably from territory to territory. In some, much of the pre-existing customary tenure and its administration was left intact, but failure to fully understand the resource tenure systems they encountered, or the lack of relevance to African situations of the European experiences that they brought with them, frequently led colonial powers to impose changes that have proved detrimental to the functioning and evolution of resource management. A frequently cited instance has been the failure to recognize the role of fallow and common pool land, classifying it as unoccupied and the property of the state (Lawry, 1989; Shepherd, 1992).

Some colonial regimes tried to bring all forest land under government control. This trend was extended and broadened during the postindependence period when central governments sought to exercise political as well as administrative control over their new nations. By creating new power centres, such as political organizations, and bureaucratic structures that reach down to the village level, governments have often reduced or altered the nature of the influence of traditional local institutions and leaders. Much political and economic authority has passed from clan and lineage leaders to the state, which has taken over responsibility for natural resource management and conflict resolution. As a result, people increasingly leave management of local tree resources to the forest department, to avoid the high social transaction costs of organizing the management of small areas of forest in such difficult and adverse circumstances (Birgegård, 1993; Lawry, 1989; Shepherd, 1992).

At the same time, woodland management has come under increased pressure from population increases and migration, the spread of settled agriculture and other economic changes. Weakened customary systems of control no longer have the flexibility to adjust to these changes. Subsidiary uses, such as the collection of fuelwood by women, that are less codified or strongly entrenched in customary tenure and rights are becoming increasingly threatened (Mortimore, 1996). Where local users have little, if any, power to exclude outsiders or arbitrate conflicts, many communal areas have been degraded or have disappeared. Encroachment, often with government support, has been widespread. Local courts and administrative units that have taken charge of conflict resolution generally do not understand indigenous tenure systems and make decisions based on other criteria (Birgegård, 1993; Shepherd, 1992).

With the decline in the effectiveness of customary communal systems, the focus has been shifting toward the household and the strengthening of individual rights. As a consequence, a large and increasing share of tree product production is now based on tree stocks on farmland under individual control. Nevertheless, people continue to rely on inputs from nearby forests in much of the region. In particular, continued access to forests provides a buffer against the shortfalls in food and income flows in periods of poor agricultural conditions or reduced-wage employment (Falconer, 1990).

Elements of customary tenure are still often present. Contemporary systems are commonly made up of "multiple forms of overlapping and interpenetrating land and resource rights that encompass both group and individual claims. In short, a plot of land may have multiple claims upon it, both group and individual, that can include rights to water, fuel, grazing, cultivation plots, and any number of other activities and [products]. These rights of access and use may vary according to season, social identity, species or type of usage" (Neumann, 1996). In a recent survey in Zimbabwe (Fortmann and Nhira, 1992), various multiple use and management arrangements were identified, with different systems of control (sacred control, pragmatic controls, civil contract, new controlling institutions and rules) for different land categories (state, commercial, communal, individual, etc.). Most of these tenurial arrangements were still evolving and adapting to a changing situation.

In many countries in the region, existing patterns of tenure and rights are now under threat from programmes to introduce individual titling in place of communal land systems, in the expectation that this will bring about improved agricultural productivity and growth. As Neumann (1996) has pointed out: "Land titling programmes, based on the relatively more rigid concept of private property, cannot address the complexity and flexibility of existing land and resource tenure." Misunderstanding of the present system and its origins thus risks doing more damage to what remains of indigenous management and use systems.

In some situations, pressures of growing shortages and increased competition for resources from outside interests have stimulated efforts to revive or establish local management systems. In parts of Mali, for instance, there has been a resurgence in interest in the strong system of communal management of local forest CPRs that had flourished until it was stifled by the increasing spread of state control in the postindependence period. This follows a change in government which, though not revoking the earlier Forestry Code that had brought all tree-bearing land under the control of the state, has reportedly recognized (1) that the Forestry Code was not effective and failed to prevent resource degradation, and (2) that local users had the capability and motivation to manage the forests more effectively (Thomson and Coulibaly, 1995).

Several governments in the region are now examining the possibilities of reversing some of the policy and legal impediments to effective local control over forest and other natural resources.

There is also growing interest in developing new initiatives that enable effective local control within the framework of contemporary political and administrative systems (e.g. Zimbabwe's CAMPFIRE programme, reviewed later in this study).

South America

In this region, much of the management of forest resources as common property has been in the Amazon basin, in the form of land and resource management systems practised by indigenous forest-dwelling groups. Their land use practices are closely linked to their social institutions and cultural perceptions of the natural and supernatural environment that governs productive activities. Rules of access and offtake are based on sophisticated knowledge of the forest's carrying capacity. Within a community, all have equal access to productive resources and knowledge, with each group regulating its members' access to productive resources and the distribution of production within the group (Chase Smith, 1995; Davis and Wali, 1993).

These traditional systems have been widely undermined by states that claim land and natural resources but are unable to control the areas in question. The insecurity this causes has encouraged exploitative use and open access situations, which in turn encourage state appropriation and privatization. Since the colonial era, countries in the region have pursued policies of encouraging settlement by colonists and ceding resources to logging, mining and other private interests. The requirement that settlers put land granted to them to productive use, and the linking of land clearance with property rights, has further undermined incentives for collective management (Ascher, 1995; Perl *et al.*, 1991; Southgate and Runge, 1990).

Indigenous user groups have therefore had to cope with a high degree of tenure insecurity (Forster and Stansfield, 1993). In modern times, most states have attempted to address some aspects of this through legislation. However, this legislation has tended to reflect successive policies of:

- protectionism (assuming that target populations are incapable of protecting themselves and, therefore, entrusting their well-being to outside agencies);
- integration (encouraging development by opening up areas to outside settlers and promising land and organizational help to indigenous populations); and
- preservation (setting aside areas for indigenous people, wildlife and the environment).

However, as Davis and Wali (1993) have pointed out, in practice such measures are often ineffective, for several reasons.

- Only a small proportion of protectionist interventions, such as creation of Indian Reserves, are fully regularized and so are often unable to prevent encroachment by outsiders.
- Integration-oriented systems, such as Native Communities, ignore traditional tenure in favour of nationally uniform models for peasant organization, such as rural syndicates or cooperatives, which often are not compatible with traditional management practices.
- Lack of legal title for Protected Areas creates insecurity against long-term encroachment by other interests (e.g. timber, ecotourism), and procedures for administration of such areas fail to involve members in decisions about their area.

Other weaknesses that contribute to the ineffectiveness of most of the solutions presently in place include costly and time-consuming validation procedures, exclusion of fallow land as 'non-tenurable', and failure to uphold law and order (Southgate and Runge, 1990). Efforts to get indigenous communities to modify their institutional structures in order to meet the requirements for legal recognition usually have not been successful and can undermine their existing structures (Chase Smith, 1995). Where indigenous institutions have been recognized, this has been based on old legislation, and the process has suffered from the bureaucratic delays associated with the implementation of the latter (Davis and Wali, 1993). Imposition of outside laws or institutional constraints on traditional arrangements has tended to aggravate or catalyze internal problems that can lead to breakdown of the latter (Richards, 1997). As has been pointed out by Davis and Wali (1993): "...it is clear that national policy-makers have had little understanding of either the dynamics of indigenous land use or the symbolic and cultural meanings which indigenous forest-dwellers give to space."

Failure to recognize indigenous land use systems, confusion of multiple overlapping rights and separation of land and tree ownership have all eroded the base of common property systems. The arguments that equate CPRs with open access enable governments to evade pressures for land reform and the need to resist incursions by vested interests (Southgate and Runge, 1994).

It also has been argued (Chase Smith, 1995) that indigenous systems are threatened by the progressive intrusion of market forces. Participating in market transactions can threaten traditional exchange systems between people and erode the reciprocal 'gift economy' in which the incentive for group cooperation is the obligation to reciprocate. The concept of accumulating individual wealth to enhance personal status conflicts with the concept of status enhanced by giving and receiving. Market pressures undermine traditional checks on extractive practices. However, some indigenous communities have managed to maintain labour reciprocity as they move to commercial use of forests, and have been able to exercise local control over extraction through traditional authorities (Richards, 1997).

Heavy immigration pressures from colonists have contributed to the failure to maintain or create common property systems (Forster and Stansfield, 1993). If colonists are entitled to stake claims to state forest land, they can come to regard all forest land as prospective private property (Dorner and Thiesenhausen, 1992). The process of sequential clearing-cropping-pasturing of successive plots by individual settlers that characterizes colonization works against collective management. However, in areas that are not under heavy settlement pressure, effective informal rules are sometimes to be found. Rudel (1995) reports situations in which settlers without formal title have developed and enforced social controls that respect not only individuals' rights to the areas they have cleared, but also their rights to draw on a larger area of surrounding uncleared forest. Thus, smallholders do not need to clear large tracts of land in order to secure their claim to it. As settlement densities increase, these informal collective arrangements tend to evolve into individual private property.

Despite the general picture of decreasingly effective common property management, there are numerous reports of indigenous communities reacting to increased outside pressures on their resources by tightening control over parts of their forest areas in order to limit their exploitation. However, such initiatives tend to be hampered by insecure tenure, substantial benefits to individual extractors, a high level of encroachment by outsiders and lack of supportive state regulations (Richards, 1997).[6]

Lessons Learned

The material reviewed so far illustrates the wide range of forms of tenure, and of coexisting and often overlapping property tenure, that still exists. In general, though, indigenous forms of management of forest and other tree resources as common property are associated with two types of land use. One is land on which swidden agriculture is practised, with cropping alternating with periods of bush and forest fallow. The other is land that provides inputs needed to sustain nearby areas of settled agriculture.

The review confirms the great extent to which common property systems that were important and widespread in the past have declined. It also shows many instances in which user communities have attempted to revive some form of collective management or introduce new or modified forms of such management. The following sections examine the implications for contemporary management of forests as common property of the information about (1) the nature and reasons for the decline in common property management, and (2) the systems that have endured or emerged.

The Decline in Management of Forests as Common Property

Much of the decline and disappearance of common property systems has come about as communities have opted for alternatives in face of economic, demographic and social change. Combinations of these factors can render collective

6 The creation of extractive reserves for rubber tappers arguably forms another type of recent common property regime. However, the excludability and indivisibility problems involved mean that in practice they are effectively privatized among individual families (McElwee, 1994).

control systems inoperable, as is illustrated for low rainfall areas in India in Boxes 3 and 4 (Jodha, 1990). Factors that contribute to such changes are increasing population pressure, market opportunities and pressures, the option of purchasing rather than producing certain goods, adoption of agricultural technologies (such as tractors) that permit cultivation of larger areas, increasing capacity to capture benefits through privatization, and changes in rural labour availability and allocation. In many situations, the circumstances favouring common property management, identified in the introductory chapter of the study, probably no longer exist or are much weaker, favouring individual private ownership or state management.

An equally important set of factors that emerges from the review as contributing to the decline in common property systems is policies, legislation and actions by agencies of the state. As McKean and Ostrom (1995) have pointed out, most common property regimes seem to have been legislated out of existence, or ignored because they were never codified, or eliminated by land reform in favour of individuals or the government. The result has been summarized by Bruce (1996) as follows: "In many parts of the world the national state has rejected or simply refused to recognize indigenous common property regimes, and by undermining them, has returned large areas to the relative chaos of open access. It has then often responded to this chaos by insisting that the state must assume control of the resource."

This would suggest that there are many situations in which conditions might favour common property management if it were not for the negative policy environment. If this interpretation is correct, then it becomes particularly important to understand how the institutional framework in a given situation affects the potential for creating conditions that are more supportive of common property systems that are appropriate for the economic, social and demographic circumstances.

Perhaps the most pervasive form of state intervention is expropriation of forest and woodland as forest reserves or some other form of state property. At a minimum, this involves replacing users' rights to the forest with a more limited set of privileges related to use of specified forest products, usually governed by restrictive regulations and exercisable at the whim of the officials of the responsible government department.

The ostensible reason why the state claims forest lands is to ensure sustainable use for environmental and economic outputs.[7] The potential value of forests as a source of rent to governments helps explain the reasons for breaking down existing management systems. As Berkes (1993) has pointed out, "open-access ... is an efficient regime for the quick conversion of resources into money. Thus it is not surprising that colonialists often dismantled communal property regimes and institutions as a prelude to establishing colonial economies."

As was made clear from much of the information reviewed, the impact of state intervention has often been intensified by failure to understand the functioning of the existing systems. The fact that the "empty" areas being claimed for the state in much of Africa were in fact lands under fallow was not recognized. Nor was the role of fallow in land use and the local economy recognized. There was a similar failure in understanding when dealing with the sophisticated use and management systems in forest areas in regions such as the Amazon and central India. This pattern of intervention based on insufficient understanding continues to the present with the drive for individual titling in areas of Africa that at present have complex, multiple, overlapping mixtures of individual and collective rights and uses.

The second form of state intervention, particularly in the postindependence era, has been the increase of government control over local activities. In recent times this has often accelerated, as those coming to power after independence try to build nations from usually diverse, fragmented and dispersed populations. The inevitable conflicts with existing power structures and allegiances encourage measures to undermine and remove previously functioning local governance and management systems, and replace them with political and bureaucratic structures and regulations. This has not been confined to forestry, but has had a particular impact in this sector because the state usually has been unable to provide effec-

7 Another reason, less frequently articulated, is to secure sparsely populated areas against claims from other countries.

tive control over such large areas. Existing systems have consequently been undermined or suppressed, but have not been replaced by an effective alternative.

State intervention has also had massive adverse impacts on common property systems through the less direct path of land reform. The huge reduction in the area of village-linked CPRs in India during the past two or three decades has come about largely through programmes allocating individual land parcels to the landless and poor. Settlement programmes in South America and land titling in Africa have had a similar impact.

However, in the areas of India described by Jodha (1990), the remaining CPRs still fill crucial gaps in resource and income flows from other resources for the poor. Moreover, much of the land being allocated to individuals is too poor to support sustainable crop agriculture without heavy investment, so often the poor are not able to retain control of the plots of such land allocated to them. In the end, they are deprived of access to CPRs and have no control over an offsetting private resource. Thus the alternatives that have displaced common property systems are not necessarily satisfactory, at least not for all. However, it is less clear whether, in the absence of land reform, the collective control systems would have been compatible with the economic, demographic and other pressures that have contributed to their decline (see Box 3).

Common Property Regimes that Have Endured or Emerged

Many studies of the indigenous common property systems that have survived through considerable periods of change identify small size, internal homogeneity, functioning local leadership and isolation from markets as important determinants of their endurance. As these are not conditions that can be created easily, because the factors are not easy to alter within the framework of resource management, they provide only limited insight into how new interventions or policies could support common property systems in less advantageous conditions (Jodha, 1990).

The factors that emerge from studies of common property regimes that have been revived or strengthened during recent times are probably more significant. Four reasons for renewed local management can be identified:

- growing shortages of forest products and other forest outputs of value to the user community (e.g. water in hill areas in Thailand),
- increased pressures from outside interests to use forest resources that are still important sources of supply to the community;
- new challenges that need, or would be more effectively handled by, collective action (e.g. the need of colonists to collaborate in maintaining infrastructure and services in lightly settled areas in the Amazon); and
- new needs or opportunities, such as the opportunity to reassert local control if government policies or practices make this possible and expedient (e.g. in Nepal in the late 1950s and again from the late 1980s).

Thus, though shortages and increasing competition often contribute to the breakdown of common property regimes, they can also, in appropriate circumstances, stimulate collective management.

From these experiences it is possible to identify a number of factors that seem to be important in explaining relative degrees of effectiveness:

- at minimum, the tacit permission or support of the state and, preferably, formal·authorization, and supportive actions by forest departments; social cohesion within the group and, preferably, experience in other forms of collective management of other local activities;
- sufficient flexibility within the community and its institution(s) to adapt to market pressures and opportunities; and
- transaction costs of organizing, implementing and monitoring a common property regime that can be kept in check and remain commensurate with the benefits of collective management.

We can extend our understanding of factors accounting for long-lasting common property systems in forestry by looking at two well-documented instances in other parts of the world. One is a situation in the Swiss alps (Netting, 1981, as cited in Ostrom, 1990). The other involves three communities in a mountain area in Japan (McKean, 1986).

Both are situations in which mountain communities manage the more productive land that is used for agriculture as private property, while the more extensive areas of poorer upland forest, meadow and wasteland are managed as common property and used for fodder, grazing, timber, etc. In both situations, tight restrictions on entry of outsiders into the user group have resulted in stable populations over long periods of time. Rules are set and modified when necessary by the group without interference by outside authorities. Adherence is controlled by officials appointed by the group and by systems of graduated penalties. Use involves some collaborative work, which helps contain the costs of monitoring and reduces disputes over distribution of benefits.

In commenting on the lessons that can be learned from these and other long-enduring systems (see Box 5), Ostrom (1990) emphasizes flexibility, dependence on internal rather than external institutions to establish and enforce rules, attention to monitoring, and rules and procedures that contribute to keeping costs low and operation of the system relatively free from conflict.

Box 5: Design Principles Illustrated by Long-enduring CPR Institutions

Clearly defined boundaries: Individuals or households who have rights to withdraw resource units from the CPR must be clearly defined, as must the boundaries of the CPR itself.

Congruence between appropriation and provision rules and local conditions: Appropriation rules restricting time, place, technology and/or quantity of resource units are related to local conditions and to provision rules requiring labour, material and/or money.

Collective-choice arrangements: Most individuals affected by the operational rules can participate in modifying the operational rules.

Monitoring: Monitors, who actively audit CPR conditions and appropriator behaviour, are accountable to the appropriators or are the appropriators.[1]

Graduated sanctions: Appropriators who violate operational rules are likely to be assessed graduated sanctions (depending on the seriousness and context of the offense) by other appropriators, by officials accountable to these appropriators, or by both.

Conflict resolution mechanisms: Appropriators and their officials have rapid access to low-cost local arenas to resolve conflicts among appropriators, or between appropriators and officials.

Minimal recognition of rights to organize: The rights of appropriators to devise their own institutions are not challenged by external governmental authorities.

Nested enterprises: For CPRs that are part of larger systems, appropriation, provision, monitoring, enforcement, conflict resolution and governance activities are organized in multiple layers of nested enterprises.

1 The term 'appropriators' refers here to those who withdraw resource units from the CPR, i.e. those who gather or harvest products for use or sale.

Source: Ostrom, 1990

Chapter 3: Case studies of contemporary collective and co-management systems

This chapter examines selected major recent and current experiences of government interventions to create or support contemporary systems of collective management of forest resources and forest products.

Nine programmes are reviewed. Each involves some form of contractual arrangement between the state and local users, designed to improve both management of the resource and the distribution of benefits from its use. In contrast with the previous chapter on indigenous systems, the focus here is thus on systems where the initiative has come from outside rather than inside the user population.

Though there are no sharp boundaries between them, these programmes may be grouped into four broad categories of forest situation.

The following assessment of these programmes focuses on factors that were identified in the previous chapters as important in explaining success or lack of success in common property management in forestry. It therefore highlights the nature and role of the CPR, the macro- and microinstitutional contexts, and the effectiveness of both local and state components of each programme.

Management of Natural Resources on Communal Lands
Land is owned by or exclusively allocated to communities, but the state historically has exercised control over forest/woodland resources on that land
- Ejido Forests, Mexico
- CAMPFIRE Wildlife Management, Zimbabwe

Management of Forestry and Agriculture on Forest Land
Forest areas where swidden agriculture is giving way to slash-and-burn and settled agriculture
- Stewardship Agreements, Philippines
- Forest Villages, Thailand

Joint or Collective Management of Areas of State Forest
Farm households still depend upon heavy inputs of green mulch, fodder, income, etc., from nearby areas of forest, and state forest resources are under pressure from local users
- Hill Community Forestry, Nepal
- Van Panchayats, Uttar Pradesh, India
- Joint Forest Management, India

Management of Collective Forestation on Village Lands
Areas of settled agriculture where new and more accessible sources of forest products are needed in order to improve local supplies and reduce pressures on remaining natural forests
- Social Forestry Village Woodlots, India
- Village Forestry, Republic of Korea

Management of Natural Resources on Communal Lands

The two case studies in this group deal with management of resources on lands over which local people had long had legal rights. In both cases, the governments had imposed substantial control over use of forest and other natural resources on these lands. Recently, moves have been initiated to transfer some control back to the community level. The studies summarize the legal and institutional changes and support measures designed to achieve this and to strengthen local management capabilities.

Ejido Forests - Mexico The rights of use to the *ejido* lands were granted to the communities (*ejidos*) after the 1910 revolution. Arable land is typically assigned to individuals but forest and pasture land is held in common. All ejidos have a common organizational structure, but each has to develop its own rules and regulations regarding exploitation, conflict resolution, benefit sharing, etc.

The ejido lands contain much of the country's forest resources and, until legislation in 1986, were in effect controlled by the government, which granted logging concessions to forest industries, some of them state-owned. The residents of the ejidos benefited very little in income or employment. A nominal stumpage fee was paid into a community development fund administered by the Ministry of Agrarian Reform, but little was transferred to the ejidos.

In the mid-1970s, peasant organizations campaigned to change the system so they could participate more directly in control and exploitation of their forests, and benefit more substantially and sustainably from the proceeds. In the mid-1980s, new legislation, culminating in the 1986 Forestry Law, transferred decision-making power over forest harvesting to the ejidos (subject to their obtaining approval for a management plan, to be drawn up by a forester). By 1988, there were at least 23 ejido organizations managing their forests in 13 states, with variable results.

The earlier arrangements usually were heavily entrenched, and those benefiting from them frequently have been reluctant to accept change. It became apparent that change would often require new institutions and the withdrawal of existing organizations. The technical assistance functions previously assumed by the state were first decentralized and then privatized, with the state reduced essentially to a supervisory role. In 1992, another Forestry Law established a national coordinating body, with regional bodies to provide fora for consultation by all interested parties.

In one of the apparently more successful of these initiatives, the Plan Piloto Forestal (PPF) in the tropical region of Quintana Roo, 10 ejidos have, since 1983, progressively taken over responsibility for management and exploitation of their forest resources (initially producing mainly chicle,[8] but now principally harvesting mahogany). At an early stage it was realized that an autonomous institutional structure would be needed to provide a single voice for dealing with the government and the market, and to provide legal and technical assistance. This was created as the Sociedad de Productores Forestales Ejidales de Quintana Roo AC (SPFEQR).

The SPFEQR provided the ejidos with the institutional mechanism to operate independently of the Ministry of Agrarian Reform, to request and be granted concessions, and to take over technical assistance responsibilities from the Ministry of Agriculture and Water Resources. At the same time, each ejido maintains an autonomous forest management unit, and all production and management decisions continue to be made by the general assembly of each ejido.

The national forestry department pays the salaries of the forestry staff now assigned to the SPFEQR and the ejidos, and, with a donor project, has helped with technical and financial assistance. Progress has also required the involvement of the state and central government on a number of occasions to resolve political and other problems that have arisen.

The PPF has already been replicated three times, and by 1995 had been extended to about 50 ejidos covering 500 000 ha in the state. Active marketing has increased prices and expanded the range of species sold, ensuring larger income flows and an ability to finance further capitalization of the enterprise. The larger ejidos with mahogany-rich resources have been able to invest in processing. However, those with a poorer resource base have often found it difficult to maintain their members' interest in forest management, which consequently has declined in favour of agriculture.

In organizing and running their operations, many ejidos have been able to draw on a long

8 A coagulated latex tapped from chicozapete trees (*Manilkara zapote*) and used in the production of chewing gum and other products.

experience with chicle cooperatives. Arrangements for distribution of benefits within communities have reflected traditional conventions such as annual rotation of posts, uniform salaries and consensual decision-making. While this has encouraged social cohesion, it has weakened business efficiency. Technical and business practices continue to show some weak points, and it is not clear yet if communities can function sustainably without at least some of the external advice and support they have been receiving.

In 1992, constitutional reform effectively privatized ejido land allocated to individuals and the rights of users of communal land. This has strengthened ejidos' legal rights to own and manage forest land, but makes it easier, if a majority of community members so wish, to clear the forest and parcel out the land. This possibility has raised fears that the reform may work against the poorer ejido members, who have fewer options and only a limited say in decisions. Queries have also been raised about the ability of ejidos to compete against the cheaper timber imported since the North American Free Trade Agreement took effect.

(Goldring, 1995; Perl *et al.*, 1991; Richards, 1991; Richards *et al.*, 1995; Rodriguez *et al.*, 1993; Snook, 1991)

CAMPFIRE - Zimbabwe The CAMPFIRE (Communal Areas Management Programme for Indigenous Resources) project in Zimbabwe has been developed in an effort to provide local communities with access to, control over and responsibility for the wildlife resources on their land. Related objectives are to empower the communities to make decisions about those resources, to ensure that they receive an equitable share of the benefits from exploitation of their resources, and to support institutional strengthening at the community level.

Historically, wildlife management in Africa has been controlled by governments. A focus on preservation and the revenue-generating potential of wildlife, and the creation of parks and buffer zones in pursuit of these objectives, has led to state intervention and top-down control of wildlife exploitation and management even on land held under communal tenure. Most moves to involve local communities have resulted at best in passive participation, with communities rarely politically or legally empowered, because governments see devolution of control over land and resources as a threat to their authority.

The initiative to bring about active local participation through CAMPFIRE grew out of permissive legislation in the 1980s that allowed revenues derived from wildlife to accrue to District Councils rather than central government. The programme became operational in two districts in 1988, and by 1994 it had been extended to 22 districts. It is implemented by the Department of National Parks and Wildlife Management, in collaboration with the University of Zimbabwe, local and international NGOs, and an association of District Councils set up for this purpose.

CAMPFIRE is initiated in an area by its District Council, or by member communities working through their District Council, applying for and being granted authority to run the programme. Management is handled by council and community wildlife committees that receive training in fiscal and resource management. Programme activities involve planning of local hunting and fire management, control of poaching and other wildlife-related activities, and allocation of income. The main element is the generation of revenue through hunting concessions, trophy fees and safari operations developed through contracts or joint ventures with private sector operators.

In some areas, CAMPFIRE has had considerable success, increasing household and communal revenues, reducing poaching and problems from interactions with wildlife, and strengthening local conservation attitudes and practices. Success has usually required complex negotiation over group membership, household definition and revenue-sharing procedures, and is more likely to occur in areas with the poorest agricultural prospects, low populations, abundant wildlife and few alternative sources of income.

The principal problems have stemmed from the reluctance of District Councils to devolve real responsibility and authority to the communities or to distribute their full share of the revenue to the latter. The programme has become primarily a source of revenue for District Councils, which have often failed to involve the communities in planning and management to the degree called for in the CAMPFIRE agreements. The tendency for councils to capture wildlife revenue is being reinforced by the squeeze on their revenue from the central government as the latter implements austerity measures in pursuit of a structural adjustment strategy.

These problems can be aggravated by the differences that exist between the modern administrative structure of District Councils, and the reality of the local social and economic situations. Administrative boundaries may not coincide with the traditional boundaries of communities, and traditional leadership may not be represented satisfactorily in elected bodies. Councils typically preside over areas that are ecologically diverse and have different potentials and different problems with utilizing wildlife, differences that are not adequately reflected in council management plans and practices. Proposals to devolve authority from District Councils down to wards have been countered by arguments that wards are also units of local government and would be unlikely to solve the problems at the interface between state and community institutions.

As the success of the activities is sensitive to the balance between costs and benefits, attention also has focused on a number of economic issues. Operating costs, in particular the costs of the management structures created at the district level, have tended to be high. Within communities, there have been difficulties in creating benefit distribution mechanisms that reflect the differential impacts of costs related to wildlife management, e.g. compensating those who bear the brunt of costs of animal damage to crops.

It has been argued that these are primarily operational problems rather than flaws in the concept underlying CAMPFIRE, and that they can be overcome by drawing on the following lessons.

- CAMPFIRE is an option that should be considered only where farmers are in agreement that wildlife management is a competitive form of land use.
- To be successful it must bring together ownership, management, cost and benefit of wildlife in one institutional unit (i.e. authority as well as responsibility must rest with the communal regime).
- The scale of operation needs to be small enough for the managing community to be able to ensure adherence to rules, primarily through informal group pressure.
- The authorized local management entity needs to have the capacity to exercise control.

The CAMPFIRE experience has been developed for a particular situation. However, the progress it has made in devolving authority and control over wildlife resources to user communities has raised the possibility that it could provide a model for local management of other woodland resources in comparable institutional settings.

(IIED, 1994; Murombedzi, 1992; Murphree, 1996; Scoones and Matose, 1993)

Joint or Collective Management of Areas of State Forest

Several of the more interesting examples of recent initiatives come from hill and other forested areas in Nepal and India, where forest departments have reversed the usual trend of increasing control over large tracts of degraded forests and have given specific powers to local institutions. In each case reviewed here, local people had some usufructuary rights that had been progressively reduced or restricted. However the forest department was unable to exercise effective control over the areas where it had legal control, and productivity was declining. At the same time, villagers had difficulty securing the forest products they needed. In order to resolve these problems, local control and authority were increased under agreements in which villagers would get a much larger share of future produce if they managed the forests to meet agreed conservation and sustainability criteria. The cases focus on the policy, legal and institutional changes initiated by governments in order to implement this, and on the implications and impacts at the community and user group level.

Hill Community Forestry - Nepal

In the middle hills of Nepal, a generally roadless region where villagers remain extremely isolated because of the nature of the terrain, local supplies of arboreal fodder, green mulch, fuel and timber have always been, and remain, central to the local agricultural systems. Historically, forests were controlled under various forms of tenure, some feudal, some in the name of the state and some communal. Though many landowners sought to generate revenue from use of the forests, local people were generally allowed free access to products that they needed for their own use.

An overthrow of the feudal system in the 1950s brought an end to the privileges and power of the landowner classes. Their forests were brought under the control of the state, under the Private Forests Nationalization Act of 1957. Since the government was unable to exercise its authority in the remoter regions, this control was circumvented by many owners. Where there was strong local leadership, forests remained effectively under local control, and, as was mentioned earlier, many of the indigenous communal management systems date from this period. However, uncertainties over ownership, aggravated by concerns raised by the cadastral survey and formal demarcation of private land, led to widespread exploitation of forests and conversion of forest land to agriculture.

By the mid-1970s, forest depletion and degradation were leading to shortages of forest products in some areas. In 1978, the government passed legislation enabling substantial amounts of public forest land in the middle hills to be handed over to local communities to manage, in recognition of the practical difficulties of managing the country's dispersed forest resources through the forest department. Local management was to be achieved through the *panchayats*, the lowest level of political and administrative organization. Panchayats would enter into agreements with the government to manage local areas under agreed forest management plans. Participating panchayats were required to set up a Panchayat Forest Committee with the forest department providing an infrastructure of nurseries and extension staff, and financing for locally recruited nursery foremen and forest watchers.[9] Funding and technical assistance were provided by a number of donors.

Progress was slow at first. Initially, the programme had to overcome the villagers' widespread suspicion that it was just another way of abrogating their customary rights. Panchayats usually proved to be unsuitable bodies to undertake local forest management, as the areas they administered seldom coincided with user group boundaries. Though forest management committees were formed, they seldom functioned as representative discussion and decision-making bodies. Management plans designed by the forest department to increase productivity tended to be neither technically acceptable nor intelligible to villagers. Cumbersome bureaucratic procedures surrounding authorization of the handover of forest lands to communities, the granting of permission to harvest and sell produce from communal forest areas, and the slow payment of revenue to the community discouraged local involvement.

Subsequently, a succession of adjustments has moved the government programmes in the direction of the indigenous control and management systems that many communities within the middle hill areas were practising spontaneously. The indigenous systems were typically based on user groups, rather than whole villages, wards or panchayats. User groups established simple and usually conservative management rules based on limit ing harvesting by area, size or quantity of product, or by time of year, with the rules being enforced by means of forest watchers and social sanctions.

Following passage of the Decentralization Act in 1982, the government initiated a series of measures that shifted the focus from the panchayat to the user group,[10] with more authority and responsibility progressively devolving to these groups. An important step in refining the system has been the recognition that there are different categories of users interested in a particular forest resource. These range from primary users who depend on the resource for all of their forest product needs, to secondary users who use it for a more limited purpose, and to other interest groups, such as collectors of medicinal products. Experience also showed that user group motivation (or lack of motivation) to engage in participatory forest management is related to factors such as manageable size, quality of resource and technical ease of management.

[9] The programme also encouraged collective planting of denuded communal land. Much less progress has been made with this than with the development of collective management of existing forests. The programme also supported planting by farmers on their own land.

[10] Replaced after the abolition of the panchayat system by elected Village Development Committees.

User groups now develop their own operational plans, set the prices at which the produce is sold and determine how surplus income is spent. Groups are being established at an increasing rate and are building steadily on the authority they have acquired through legal control over the resource. User groups are now coming together and sharing experiences in networking workshops and range-level planning exercises. Some are also becoming general local development organizations and are registering as NGOs in order to gain greater access to government services.

By early 1996, there were 3000 user groups, managing 200 000 ha (Department of Forests, 1996). The experience of the 1970s and 1980s has been entrenched in the 1989 Master Plan for the Forestry Sector. This has formalized much of the experimentation with new institutional formats, and the user group approach was given legal authority in the 1993 Forest Act. Ownership of the land remains with the state, but trees legally belong to user groups, though the state reserves the right to take back possession of the community forest if the terms and conditions of handover are not met. The state's role is thus defined as being that of a regulatory authority only. Management control rests solely with the users of the resource.

The approach to formalizing a collective system for managing local forest areas has proceeded further in Nepal than in most countries. There has been a steady decentralization of forest department staff and functions to the districts, and authority to transfer forest areas to user groups now rests with the District Forest Officer. Training has helped remove many of the impediments to and reservations about the process that forest staff had experienced earlier. Nevertheless, given the importance that control represents in terms of political and economic power, and the role that patronage and hierarchical structures play in the bureaucracy, it must be expected that further progress will still encounter some reluctance and even resistance from within the forestry establishment.

(Arnold and Campbell, 1986; Department of Forests, 1996; Fisher, 1989; Gilmour and Fisher, 1991; Hobley, 1996a; Malla, 1994; Molnar, 1981; Talbott and Khadka, 1994)

Van Panchayats - Uttar Pradesh, India The Van (Forest) Panchayats of the Garwhal and Kumaon regions of the Uttar Pradesh hills represent one of the largest, longest running and most diverse experiments in collective systems of forest management developed in cooperation with the state. They were introduced in the 1920s by the civil administration after a prolonged period of intense agitation by villagers against a major expansion of British control over forest resources in the Uttar Pradesh hills. In order to resolve this dispute, a category of forest of little or no commercial importance was established to provide for local needs, to be managed by a village body (*Van Panchayat*) in accordance with a set of government regulations and legislation. The forest department retained control over timber and resin management in these areas, but the village received any profit made from sale of these products. Though many of these village bodies have ceased to function, new Van Panchayats continue to be formed. In 1995 it was reported that in the Kumaon region there were nearly 3000 Van Panchayats controlling 35 percent of the forests.

The panchayat body selects a leader from among its members, establishes management rules consistent with the authority established by the Forest Panchayat Act of 1931 (amended in 1976), establishes measures to ensure enforcement of these rules and manages the disbursement of funds that accrue from forest activities. The collection of a tax, either at harvest or monthly, reinforces the legitimacy of the local institution and provides the necessary funds at the village level.

Individual Van Panchayats have adopted a wide range of rules and regulations, which have evolved considerably over time in response to changes in the local situation. Where fair elections to the village bodies are held, most villagers have reported that they consider the management of the forest good and the distribution of the forest products equitable.

Forest resources are scarce in much of the region and there is competition among panchayats for forest products. Encroachment and illegal felling are the two main problems, especially if the first cases go unpunished. All the successful Van Panchayats have guards (paid in grain or cash) or rotate the responsibility for protection among households. Smaller panchayats that cannot afford to support a guard have difficulty preventing theft, open grazing and encroachment.

The focus in most Van Panchayats has been on production and distribution of annual products such as grasses and leaf fodder, apparently partly due to the degraded state of the original resource, but also due to delays and impediments in releasing the Van Panchayat's share of the proceeds from the resin tapping and the sale of timber controlled by the forest department. Where the level of annual use is kept to a reasonable level, natural regeneration has led to significant improvements in productivity. In many cases, however, the heavy demand for forest products has simply meant that harvesting has been shifted to other forest areas.

Opinions on the success of Van Panchayats vary widely, but key factors for such success as has been achieved appear to include the following:

- confidence in government mechanisms for adjudicating boundary disputes and larger-scale external incursions;
- confidence in leadership of the Van Panchayat (e.g. open elections if there is no longer a traditional leadership);
- ability to support a guard system against encroachment and illegal felling;
- internal rules that ensure equitable distribution of benefits and compliance with the rules; and
- a rule-making mechanism that allows rules to be changed as needed.

However, over the years, successive amendments to the regulations stemming from the Forest Panchayat Act, and changes in the manner in which they are interpreted and applied, have reduced the authority of Van Panchayats to enforce their rules. Now they can impose fines only with the consent of the rule breaker or with the permission of government officials or the judiciary. With the capacity of government services to provide assistance also becoming increasingly constrained, enforcement has tended to become more difficult and costly. While villagers are usually confident of their ability to control the use of relatively low-value annual products, the control of infringements involving higher stakes is reported to be problematic in some Van Panchayats.

(Agrawal, 1994 and 1996; Ballabh and Singh; 1988; Guha, 1983 and 1985; Saxena, 1987; Tripathi, 1987; Vidyarthi, 1987)

Joint Forest Management - India Joint Forest Management (JFM) developed from the experience of the Social Forestry programmes of the 1980s, and was intended to avoid some of the weaknesses and failures of the latter.[11] To this end, JFM moved collective forestry from panchayat and revenue lands to forest lands, on which competing claims should be fewer and forest departments would have a clearer remit.

The shift to JFM also reflected growing recognition that the earlier programmes had not kept forests from being exploited to meet local needs, and that the state does not have the capacity to control use and conservation of such resources without the cooperation of those who use them. The new initiative, therefore, built on a number of state- or project-level initiatives of the 1970s and 1980s that had incorporated such a strategy, with some apparent success. Of these, the one that attracted the most attention was a programme of Village Protection Committees in West Bengal.

West Bengal The Village Protection Committees (VPCs) of West Bengal emerged in an area where most of the land was previously a mixed forest dominated by sal (*Shorea robusta*), which had been substantially altered by heavy cutting and more recent plantations. The VPCs had their origin in a pilot project started by foresters at Aribari in the early 1970s, designed to encourage villagers to stop using forest land for fuelwood cutting and cattle grazing, in return for guaranteed employment. Participating villagers were offered preferential access in their protected area to minor forest products such as sal and tendu leaves, and subsequently a 25 percent share of the income from sal poles and timber was added to their benefit.

The VPC members thus take responsibility for more of the protection and control of harvesting, in return for a substantially greater share of the

[11] See the section on Social Forestry Village Woodlots in India, below.

eventual proceeds from the resource. Benefits go directly to specific users and are not redistributed by intermediary organizations. However, the scheme involves effective closure of large tracts of the forest for a period of years, which can create considerable hardship for those villagers who previously depended on collecting activities for income and fuel.

Despite the lack of a legal basis for the programme prior to a government order in 1989, nearly 1300 VPCs had been organized by that year. By 1992, the number had grown to 2300, covering 320 000 ha of forest. Originally the villages were chosen by the forest department, but the selection process has gradually given a greater voice to local panchayats. Initially, the forest department and local political leaders had a dominant role in determining the composition and running of the committees. Since a second government order in 1990 opened membership to all, most, if not all, households usually belong to the VPC, which selects its own officials (though the panchayat and the forest department are still empowered to determine which families are eligible to benefit from the programme).

Once VPCs had been established in the first 11 villages, VPCs have been organized and managed with no external financial or organizational assistance. It has therefore been a much less costly process than most collaborative management systems initiated in recent years. The approach has been most successful in villages on the border of extensive tracts of degraded forest land, where the forest-to-household ratio is relatively high and benefits accrue from minor forest products at a relatively early stage. As more areas approach harvesting age, it has become apparent that attention needs to be given to control of harvesting and to the level and distribution of proceeds. Forest department overhead charges on the first lots to be harvested and sold were high and, because the 25 percent share assigned to the communities is based on net income, their returns have been low.

Problems of boundaries between villages and of protecting the village resource from poaching by outsiders have been emerging, in addition to problems of devising production options for areas without sal forest, and these have underlined the need for a more effective microplanning process. There has also been a lag in registration of older VPCs because it is a time-consuming process. A need to modify bureaucratic procedures for convening VPC meetings has also been identified. Working groups made up of forest department, NGO and research institution staff have proven helpful in attempts to rectify these and other operational issues.

JFM as a National Programme[12]

On the strength of this and other encouraging experiences, the government of India issued a circular to state governments in June 1990 recommending the adoption of Joint Forest Management. The main features of this circular are summarized in Box 6. By 1995, 15 states had adopted such collaborative programmes involving local communities in the management and protection of forest lands in return for rights to use specified forest products.

This huge programme has attracted much attention in other countries and regions, as well as in India, and has been more closely examined than most. Though many of the individual initiatives in different states are still at an early stage, and have met with variable success, a number of lessons of general relevance have begun to emerge.

The strengthened claim on benefits from forest use provided by JFM generally improves the position of users, but this is not always the case. For example, a JFM arrangement may regularize earlier de facto arrangements that provided a very inequitable allocation of the resource among those involved. Indeed, there could be risk of disenfranchisement for those who benefited from earlier informal arrangements, and there is some evidence of marginalized groups being left worse off by the new arrangements. In addition, questions have arisen about how consistent the interventions are with the patron-client relationships that are so important in Indian villages, and about their impact on gender relationships. Issues can also arise about the claims of different categories of users of forest products from a particular resource. Should those adjacent to forests have priority in allocation of forest benefits over those further away, when the latter may be more reliant on this usage than the former?

[12] This discussion draws in particular on the review study *Participatory forestry: The process of change in India and Nepal* (Hobley, 1996a).

Box 6: Key Features of the June 1990 Government of India Circular "Involvement of Village Communities & Voluntary Agencies in Regeneration of Degraded Forests"

- JFM should involve an 'arrangement' between the village community (i.e. the 'beneficiaries'), NGOs and the state forest department. The selected area of forest is to be managed in accordance with a working scheme approved by the state government and prepared "in consultation with the beneficiaries." The working scheme is to cover such matters as steps for inducement of natural regeneration, seeding, soil conservation methods, fire protection, maintenance of boundaries, weeding, tending, thinning, etc.

- Beneficiaries should be entitled to usufructuary rights to such items as grass, loppings and minor forest products in accordance with conditions set by the state. They may also be given a share of the proceeds from the sale of trees when they mature. They may also plant fruit trees "that would fit in with the overall scheme of afforestation."

- Only people who are willing to participate and who are organized in groups specifically for forest protection are to be made beneficiaries and thereby granted access and benefits. As an example, the circular mentions village panchayats or forest committees. However, whatever form it takes, the programme is to be focused on communities or user group subsets; the circular states explicitly that the access and benefits are not to be granted to individuals.

- Neither the beneficiaries nor any NGO may acquire ownership or lease rights over the land in question. No grazing or agriculture is allowed on the site.

- Ideally, the selected site should be free from the claims of anyone who is not a beneficiary. In other words, sites that are burdened by rights, privileges or concessions previously granted to anyone who is not part of the beneficiary group (e.g. someone from a distant village) are not preferable for JFM. Alternatively, the circular states that, for any given site, anyone who currently has a claim to forest produce should be given the opportunity to join the beneficiary group.

- The work of the beneficiaries is to be closely supervised by the Forest Department. If the work has been done in an unsatisfactory manner, "the usufructuary benefits should be withdrawn without paying compensation to any one for any work that might have been done prior to it."

Source: Lindsay, 1994

One recent study of these issues suggests that JFM is likely to be effective and appropriate if the user group and its forest area meet the following criteria: close physical proximity; prior or current formal or informal rights; high forest dependency; perceptions of resource scarcity; indigenous organizational forms of resource management; traditional socio-religious forest values; and strong local leadership (Sarin, 1993). Another study emphasizes the importance for success of JFM of a resource capable of providing a sufficient flow of benefits, the share of benefits between government and user group, and benefits that are commensurate with the costs the latter has to incur (Hobley, 1996a).

Another set of issues concerns the functioning of the communal or user group institutions authorized to be the local management body under a JFM agreement. There are reservations about panchayats assuming this role because, though they are elected, the power to make decisions usually rests with those with local political, economic or social power, and with the supervising bureaucracy. Panchayats are also generally too large to be effective as managers of small forest areas that serve the needs of particular parts of the panchayat constituency.

Therefore, JFM frequently requires the creation of a separate forest management body at the local level. However, it is difficult to do this in a participatory and democratic fashion that adequately represents the views of its constituent users. A particular issue in this respect is the effect of the considerable measure of control over such bodies by the forest department. The latter retains the right to dissolve forest committees if it thinks the committees have contravened the regulations, but is not accountable in any way that would enable committees to question its actions. The presence of forest officials in these groups can also militate against their ability to act independently.

Adapting to JFM also creates problems within forest departments. It has long been recognized that the shift from their traditional role of managing and protecting state forests to a role supporting outsiders who manage and use forests raises fundamental issues for foresters of organization, procedures, skills and attitudes. There has therefore been much focus on training and institution building. Now it is becoming evident that JFM can create more fundamental problems of conflict with the patron-client and rent-seeking relationships within public service organizations that are often the real determinants of institutional behaviour in forest departments. It is argued that, as long as JFM is seen as unlikely to provide the same basis for power and status within the department as control over a large area of forest territory, it will hold little appeal to many foresters.

Nevertheless, as is illustrated in Box 7, experience with JFM has already induced considerable adaptation and change in the right directions. There are also growing signs that, particularly among younger staff, the culture within forest departments is becoming more responsive to the underlying approach and principles.

Some of the analysis of the JFM experience also points to problems caused by lack of legal support for the programme, which is based on the 1990 central government circular and resolutions by state governments. No enabling legislation has been enacted, even though it has been argued that JFM appears to be in contradiction to current legislation, such as the Forest (Conservation) Act of 1980. This weakens the JFM initiative and has

Box 7: Changes in JFM Regulations and Practices in Haryana Brought About by Government Resolutions

From	To
[Forest department] providing technical and managerial inputs	Building technical and managerial competence in the people
Rigid allocation norms for forest areas to be protected by FPCs[1]	Forest area defined on the basis of natural features and after consultation with neighbouring village representatives and intra-village groups
Having each household as a unit member	Two adults as members of the FPC (one male, the other female)
From a fixed managing committee membership size	The society may co-opt any other technical or respected person as a non-voting member after passing a general body resolution
An umbrella-sharing policy	Different percentage of shares for different commodities, i.e. 75% of share to HRMS[2], khair 25%, fuelwood/timber 50%
Forests as a starting point	Taking up required activities as a catalyst, e.g. water, grass, bamboo
Fixed percentage-sharing arrangement	75% of the yield above the base-line production goes to the HRMS as an incentive for protection
Single resolution	Site-specific JFM area rules, e.g. bamboo artisan rules
Rights to fine [rest] with the Haryana forest department	HRMS given the right to levy fines and introduce regulations; these fines go as income to HRMS
[Forest department] ranger as ex-officio Secretary	More power to the forest guard (since he has smaller areas to look after)

1 FPC: Forest Protection Committee.

2 HRMS: Hill Resource Management Society (user group institution).

Source: SPWD, 1992

Box 8: Lessons of Experience with Joint Forest Management in India[1]

- JFM provides a means whereby the state transfers some of its rights and responsibilities to locally constituted forest protection committees(FPCs). The overall benefits and incentives to support this approach are different for the state, the FPC and specific stakeholders.

- The primary objective of the process is to introduce joint management so that local perceptions are factored into decision-making. The underlying assumptions are that there is a convergence between the private incentives of forest users and the national objective of maintaining forest resources and that people will protect the forest since they have a stake in the outputs.

- Analysis suggests that this assumption is valid at the level of the FPC and that forest protection and conservation will become more effective under JFM.

- Analysis suggests that there are overall benefits to JFM in economic terms as a result of effective protection, and that in terms of revenue the economic benefits are more secure, again as a result of protection. However, for some subgroups within the FPC, the effect of better protection is to cut off access to their livelihoods. The extent to which the perceptions and values of these subgroups are factored into decision-making depends on the functioning of the FPC. The study concluded that in large, heterogeneous FPCs the poorer, less powerful groups were marginalized as a result of the institutionalization of forest management through JFM.

- The inclusion of local perceptions requires the active involvement of people in planning, management and decision-making as well as in implementation. In practice, participation has been limited to protection activities and wage labour for crop establishment. As a result, JFM appeared to be similar to other forms of 'welfare forestry' and was often seen as just another funding scheme which, with people's participation, will enable the forest department to more effectively protect the forest. This is also reflected in the observation that JFM is associated with protection and planting rather than with management and decision-making.

- The introduction of JFM has formalized the role of the community in protecting the forest. However, there is still concern that decision-making is still biased towards timber and revenue production, since the opinions of socially weak subgroups and women, whose primary interests may be for non-wood forest products, are not reflected in decision-making by the FPCs. The existing socio-economic relationships between subgroups within each FPC determine each subgroup's bargaining power. As a result of formalizing arrangements, subgroups that previously had only marginal interest in the forest now have a stake in the forest as a result of their share in revenue.

- There are positive incentives based on perceived benefits for both forest departments and FPCs under JFM. However, pre-existing contractual arrangements and uncertainties undoubtedly act as a disincentive for some FPCs.

- The underlying complexity of both biological and socio-economic relationships supports and reinforces the principles underlying JFM, that optimum resource management requires the active participation of local stakeholders within an overall regulatory framework.

1 Findings of a study for the World Bank of the incentives for Joint Forest Management.

Source: Derived from Femconsult, 1995

created uncertainty about the extent to which village forestry bodies can be empowered legally. Uncertainty also exists as to which categories of forest could be made available for JFM; most states intend to assign 'degraded forest' from categories other than Reserved Forest.

Some of these problems have arisen because of the speed and vigour with which JFM has been disseminated. Given the ecological and political diversity of India, it is very unlikely that a single JFM model would be applicable everywhere. The experience to date is bearing this out. Its relevance needs to be carefully assessed situation by situation, which should become easier as lessons of experience become clearer (e.g. the study findings summarized in Box 8).

(Hobley, 1996a; Kurup, 1996; Lindsay, 1994; Malhotra and Poffenberger, 1989; Poffenberger and McGean, 1996; Roy, 1991; Sarin, 1993; SPWD, 1992)

Management of Forestry and Agriculture on Forest Land

In much of the forest zone of the wet tropics there has been heavy encroachment of agricultural activities into the forest. The case studies that follow describe two large-scale examples of collaborative arrangements between governments and farmers in Southeast Asia. In both the Philippines and Thailand, a considerable share of the agricultural population farms on what is still classified as forest land, and the initiatives are designed to stabilize land use and maintain areas that should stay under tree cover as forest. These strategies incorporate several approaches. The focus here is on those that are centred on communal institutions and collective management.

Communal Forest Stewardship Agreements - The Philippines

The Philippines has experienced large-scale reduction and degradation of forest area because of logging and subsequent migration of farmers into the logged areas. Very large parts of the remaining forest overlap with territories of indigenous peoples. Since the late 1970s there has been increasing interest in community forestry as a means of meeting these issues. A number of different programmes have been put in place to stabilize the situation by strengthening tenurial security and access to government services for long-term residents in the upland forest areas. The rationale is that the presence of indigenous people practising suitable forms of agroforestry helps protect against destructive land use due to indiscriminate logging and in-migration by lowlanders. The programmes have been developed over time with the help of an Upland Working Group comprising government, NGO and academic/research representatives, building on the experience of earlier programmes. Issues that have arisen include overlapping of the various programmes, resistance from vested interests and the cumbersome nature of some of the bureaucratic requirements for implementation.

The largest of the present programmes is the Integrated Social Forestry (ISF) Program initiated in 1982.[13] This is centred around the concept of 'stewardship', granting exclusive rights to use and occupy land for 25 years, renewable for another 25 years, to individuals, associations and indigenous communities. Most stewardship certificates have been issued to individuals (reportedly 256 000 certificates covering almost 586 000 ha by the end of 1993). However, most interest centres on the 36 Community Forestry Stewardship Agreements (CFSAs) granted to groups, because groups are likely to be more viable and stable than individual licensees (many of whom have been selling their licences), and agreements with groups cover relatively large areas that require proportionately less administrative inputs to set up and monitor.

Early versions of the programme were weakened by the exclusion of various categories of forest, notably areas licensed to companies for which they have contractual reforestation obligations. Successive revisions have strengthened the position of stewardship license holders, but stewardship licenses still tend to be confined to degraded forest. Procedures for establishment of CFSAs remain complex. A group has to establish itself as a non-profit corporation, carry out a survey to establish its perimeter, draw up a management plan, etc., fulfilling a set of requirements it is unlikely to complete successfully without outside help and creating the risk that licensees become dependent on external support. Most successful applications have involved assistance from a NGO (but it is reported that it has been difficult to locate NGOs able to provide assistance in such a complicated bureaucratic process).

The elaborate procedures also have placed considerable burdens on the supporting government service, the Department for the Environment and Natural Resources (DENR). In addition to staff shortages, the DENR has had to face the usual problems of forest departments as they reorganize themselves to serve a supportive role, with field staff tending to view the programme more in terms of its effectiveness in meeting governmental land use objectives than in terms of empowerment of local user groups. The very rapid rate of expansion of the granting of individual certificates has also strained DENR's capacity to monitor licensee performance.

13 There are two other large programmes. Community Forestry Management Agreements are designed to encourage reforestation and are typically awarded to contractors who then hire people to do the planting. Forest Land Management Agreements allow communities to contract to manage and protect an area of forest for 25 years in return for the right to harvest timber in the area.

But there is a commitment to the concept and to proceeding with further refinement, staff training and other measures, in order to rectify such weaknesses. A 1991 decision to decentralize government services and involve local government units in the ISF Program should in due course strengthen the effectiveness of the institutional support structure. The programme has already been effective in increasing tenure security, though conflicts between indigenous and migrant groups arise, and there can be uncertainties over prior claims to the land. Moreover, concern has been expressed that CFSAs and the other agreements have the potential to provide only limited tenurial security. Ownership remains vested in the state, and CFSAs can be revoked by the DENR if the latter considers that the community has failed to comply with the terms of its CFSA. There has consequently been growing interest among long-term occupants of forest areas in Certificates of Ancestral Domain Claims, which cannot be revoked by the government, but delineation of ancestral domain perimeters by the DENR has reportedly been slow.

(Borlagdan, 1990; Gasgonia, 1991; Gibbs *et al.*, 1990; Lynch, 1992; Lynch and Talbott, 1995; Plantilla, 1991; Sabban, 1992; Seymour and Rutherford, 1990)

Forest Villages - Thailand

In recent decades, Thailand has experienced rapid and sustained reduction in forest cover. Until recently, the country's vigorous economic growth was accompanied by heavy logging and expansion of agriculture into large areas of forests. An estimated one-fifth of the area presently under agriculture is within the boundaries of land legally classified as forests. This expansion is the result of in-migration into upland forest-dwelling populations practising swidden agriculture, and of encroachment by lowland farmers seeking additional land.

The government has responded to this reduction and degradation of the forest resource, and accompanying erosion and other environmental damage, with a number of measures designed to stabilize the land use situation, improve the productivity and sustainability of agriculture on sites suitable for crop production, and retain or restore forest cover on critical non-agricultural areas. These measures have been characterized by expansion of the area classified as state forest lands and increasing control over activities by those present within these areas. The focus has been on confining local activities to 'production' forests, excluding all activity from the very large areas now classified as parks or as other categories of conservation area.

An early component of this drive was the forest village programmes run by the Royal Forest Department (RFD) and other government agencies. The objective in such programmes was to regroup people already farming inside the forest into villages, in order to facilitate provision of infrastructure and services, stabilize the area under cultivation and encourage reforestation. Each village household was allocated a plot of arable land that could be cultivated for a specified period, supported by extension services to encourage farmers to adopt agroforestry systems and grow tree crops. In addition, employment was provided to villagers in adjacent reforestation and other forest management activities. A second government programme allocated land and temporary land use rights (STK) certificates to settlers in existing villages within the forests.

First initiated in the mid-1970s, the process of creating forest villages was expanded considerably in the mid-1980s, in response to the perceived urgency of the situation in the forest areas. This expansion encountered a number of the difficulties that forest departments are likely to meet in initiating local collective management of forest resources, and in coming to terms with the new concerns and approaches this entails. Much of the subsequent research and experimentation to improve the programmes consequently has focused on creating a more decentralized structure, training staff to work with villagers and identifying effective village-level institutions to work with.

There have been difficulties in persuading people to resettle in designated villages, as land allotments were generally smaller than the areas they already occupied, and funds were sometimes insufficient to provide adequate support to farmers in the establishment phase. The tree crops recommended by the programmes were often unattractive to farmers, particularly when the plots of land available were insufficient to meet subsistence food needs. Uncertainties over tenure were frequent, because of competing claims by those already settled in the area based on informal systems of tenure, and complex and often confusing legislation relating to land rights and use. In many areas, a continued influx of outsiders seeking allocations of land led to population densities in excess of what could be sustained on the arable areas available. The mixture of local and migrant populations often created highly factionalized villages, making it difficult for village committees to command support from all sections of the community.

Consequently, progress has been variable. Where villages have not been subjected to disruptive population and social pressures, encouraging progress has sometimes been made. This has been facilitated by formation of interdisciplinary and inter-agency working groups that have brought academic and NGO social science experts together with the foresters in the RFD. However, the village forestry programme has been costly, and the focus has increasingly shifted to the National Forest Land Allotment Project, which assigns rights to use forest land to individuals rather than communities.

(Amyot, 1988; Anan Ganjanapan, 1995; Chuntanaparb *et al.*, 1993; Hafner and Apichatvullop, 1990; Lynch and Talbott, 1995; Potisoontorn, 1990; Pragtong, 1988; Pragtong and Thomas, 1990)

Management of Collective Forestation on Village Lands

The case studies in this section describe two very large national programmes in which governments intervened to encourage communities to create new communal tree resources on their own land. In both cases this was precipitated by concern to reduce excessive pressures on remaining natural forests, and to do so by finding solutions that enabled rural people to meet their needs for fuelwood and other forest products themselves. Both involved attempts to develop new or modified community-level institutions to manage the activities, and the development and delivery of an extensive package of facilitating and support measures.

Social Forestry Village Woodlots - India

One of the largest interventions designed to increase the production of forest products on communal lands and strengthen local collective management has been the programme of communal woodlots established under Social Forestry programmes and projects in India. Social Forestry had its origins in the country in 1976, when a report of the National Commission of Agriculture recommended growing trees on lands accessible to village people in order to reduce the pressures on production forests caused by mounting rural demands for fuel, grazing and other forest products. This was to be achieved in a number of ways, one of which was to establish woodlots on non-arable communal land, to be managed collectively by the user community, through the panchayat system. Initiated in most states in the early 1980s, the programme expanded very rapidly.

The woodlots have been established mainly on village lands, and other uncultivated government lands available to villagers for communal use (e.g. revenue lands), in the drier plain areas of the country. Traditionally the main role of such common pool resources has been to complement the highly variable level of private agricultural production, by providing a major source of fodder, food and saleable products. This is especially important during extended periods of drought.

During recent decades much of the cultivable common land has been reduced by the land allocations to the rural poor discussed in the previous section, and by encroachment. Much of the rest of the common land is of low productivity. Although there are substantial regional differences, communal lands have generally been reduced to small areas, averaging 20 ha per village, and are typically heavily degraded and under open access usage. As a consequence, Social Forestry programmes in several states encountered shortages of available plantable land. Another consequence has been that the area of woodlot available to a community is often too small to contribute significantly to local needs.

The woodlots were usually established by the state forest departments, and the village lands to be planted were frequently transferred into the temporary control of that department for this purpose. Planning of the woodlot was intended to be carried out in conjunction with the local government body, the panchayat or some other community-level body, which was to take over responsibility for management in accordance with rules prescribed by the forest department and a management plan drawn up jointly with the latter. Benefits were to be split between the forest department and the community.

Under forest department management, the projects have created primarily tree stocks and wood products to be sold, with few intermediate products, such as fuelwood and grass, that previously were harvested from the areas and used by villagers. There is widespread evidence that village and panchayat bodies now perceive the Social Forestry woodlots primarily as significant sources of communal income, rather than as sources of produce to meet village needs. For this reason, there is usually a preference for auctioning the output, rather than selling it at preferential rates or distributing it free. The main benefit to the poor has usually been from the wage employment created, often on a considerable scale.

Although many of the woodlots have been in existence for quite a few years, there has been reluctance on the part of the panchayats to assume control. This seems to reflect a number of factors.

- Control entails financial responsibilities that villages and panchayats have difficulty meeting, such as, at a minimum, hiring watchers to protect the woodlot. Sometimes the budgetary implications are much more burdensome. In one state, for example, the panchayat had to pay a deposit equal to the floor value of the produce in the woodlot before taking it over.
- Woodlot management plans, village forest rules, etc., are often complex and unclear, and require skills and experience that panchayats do not possess. Very few communities have any experience in managing anything remotely resembling a woodlot, and the task of acquiring the necessary skills is complicated by management systems that reflect forest departments' technical approach to forestry.
- Continued involvement of the forest department discourages local bodies from taking over and encourages them to opt for extending forest department management. Handover arrangements commonly empower forest departments to exercise considerable control and involvement, and to retain a share of the revenue. As this is often allied with pressures on forest departments to meet very ambitious Social Forestry planting targets, they are frequently reluctant to hand over effective control.
- Lack of local interest in the woodlots because of their small size (relative to local needs), difficulties in ensuring satisfactory distribution of benefits, and uncertainties about their status and access to the benefits are additional factors.

Some of these problems reflect the lack of dialogue between forest departments and villagers concerning the purpose of and arrangements for the woodlots. The literature reports an almost universal failure to precede woodlot establishment with effective public discussion. There have been frequent reports of villagers being unaware that the woodlot had been established for the community; it was a 'government woodlot.' Often even village and panchayat officials have appeared unaware that a woodlot was to be handed over to them, nor were they aware of the implications of such a transfer. Where people have been aware of this, there usually has been lack of belief that the produce would be distributed within the community; most people did not expect any share of the final output.

The programme has also suffered from an uncertain legal situation. Social Forestry initiatives in some locations have been legally questionable, for example, using land on which legislation prohibited the growing of trees. In other situations, existing legislation that could legitimize Social Forestry actions has not been implemented. As a result, the legal status of the woodlots is often unclear, and the rights of prospective users are seldom secured by a legal document.

Though successful in increasing the productivity of the sites used and in generating a resource of considerable value to the communities, the interventions have had a different outcome from that intended.

- Use of the common land has shifted from producing products for local use to generating income for use by the community as a whole.
- Government involvement in management has in practice increased rather than decreased.
- Costs per unit of output have been high.

Though the tens of thousands of woodlots that have been established under the programme continue to be managed, the focus of support for local collectively managed forestry in India has shifted from woodlots outside the forest to the programmes of joint management within the forest that were reviewed earlier in this chapter.

(Arnold and Stewart, 1991; Chambers *et al.*, 1989; Jodha, 1986 and 1990; World Bank/USAID/GOI, 1988)

Village Forestry - Republic of Korea

The reforestation carried out by Village Forestry Associations (VFAs) in Korea represents one of the most successful examples of collective action by groups of forest product users working with the support of the state. During the 1970s and early 1980s, 643 000 ha of denuded land were replanted under the programme. The programme is also notable for the range and extent of prior planning and preparation that accompanied it, and because it dealt with private rather than public land.

The village forestry programme was initiated by the government in response to growing shortages of fuelwood and mounting problems of erosion, flooding and downstream damage to agriculture as hillsides were stripped bare by harvesting for fuel and timber. As 73 percent of forest land was in private ownership, and many private landholdings were small, any move to improve the situation had to focus on the local level and be based on local involvement.

The government initiative to encourage and support village-level reforestation built upon a tradition of forestry cooperatives. These were voluntary organizations operating in many areas to protect local forest resources, with varying degrees of effectiveness. The forestry programme in the 1970s was also created within the broader structure of the Saemaeul Undong, or New Community Movement, established in 1970 as a framework for collective self-help actions of all kinds. It had evolved in response to village-level changes, including land reform that turned tenants into landowning farmers, a weakening of the clan structure that had earlier provided the basis for village cooperation, and the emergence of more modern and egalitarian forms of village government. Saemaeul Undong projects were to be decided by consensus, and they were to involve activities for the common benefit of the village rather than the interests of particular villagers, and to reflect the particular situation and potentials of the village.

VFAs were established in all villages, and were grouped at county level into forestry associations (FAU), which in turn were members of a national federation (NFFAU). The rationale for establishing this network was that a non-governmental organization would be more effective than a government agency in mobilizing villagers to cooperate. The Office of Forestry, which was relocated to the Ministry of Home Affairs to give it access to local government resources and powers, provided technical backstopping and funding. New legislation and regulations required that forestry should be the main land use on lands with a slope of more than 36 degrees, and empowered the Office of Forestry to require landowners unable to reforest lands falling under this law to make that land available to VFAs to reforest on a cost-sharing basis.

Heads of all households in a village were members of their VFA. VFA activities benefited from subsidized credit, but members had to contribute their labour (with benefits being allocated proportionately). The technical packages introduced were strongly oriented towards short-term results and income generation, with planting of fruit and timber species as well as fuelwood, and an array of commercial activities (e.g. contracting nursery activities to village groups, employment in related government watershed protection works, and encouragement of production and marketing of mushrooms and other non-wood products).

A significant feature of the programme was its holistic nature. The Koreans set out to tackle all aspects of the fuelwood problem, while at the same time devising solutions that contributed more widely to rural welfare. Specific factors identified as having contributed to its success include:

- an incremental or step-by-step approach, with emphasis on results and identification of realistic village potentials at each stage;
- a blend of top-down and bottom-up planning, with emphasis on cooperation between government and citizens;
- attention to development of appropriate technology, technical assistance and extension, with timely delivery of needed inputs;
- financial and other assistance geared to self-help to avoid problems of village dependence on outside support; and
- formulation and application of strong, clear laws and regulations that empowered and provided authority to the VFAs and involved villagers in policing activities and preventing unauthorized use of the resources (Gregersen, 1982).

The programme thus contained strong elements of both government pressure and incentives to get it started, but as its effectiveness became evident at the village level it acquired a momentum of its own. Subsequently, large scale rural-to-urban migration in the 1980s, and the rapid rise in rural incomes and access to electric power and other services, greatly reduced the demand for fuelwood, so the programme has had to be radically restructured in favour of timber crops and much less labour intensive inputs.

(Gregersen, 1982; Oh, 1988)

Chapter 4: Assessing the implications of past and ongoing experience

A Framework for Analysis

To recapitulate, common pool resource use occurs on lands under various customary and formal tenure arrangements. Thus, communal management may be based on CPRs or be vested in communal institutions with rights to use private or state property. There may be multiple use, for different products or by different groups, at different times of the year. In practice, resources are often held in overlapping combinations of private, state, common pool resource management and open access regimes (see Box 9). Common property management systems for such resources therefore usually need to be based on recognition that the system needs to accommodate the concerns of more than one participating interest group (Campbell, 1990).

Given such diversity and variation from situation to situation and over time, there can be no universal models. As Ostrom (1994) has stated: "any single, comprehensive set of formal laws intended to govern a large expanse of territory and diverse ecological niches is bound to fail in many of the habitats where it is supposed to be

Box 9: Patterns of Tenure and Rights in India

In India ... all tenure is joint. More specifically, all land[s] - but especially forest, grazing, and fallow lands - have overlapping rights. These overlapping rights are both de jure and de facto, and are made particularly complicated by the frequent overlap of both kinds of rights. While there are often predominant assignments of these rights, or principal 'owners', these often refer to particular products or usage rights which may overlap on the same piece of land. Thus, tenure or property rights on the same tract of land also differs by product or usage. It is not surprising therefore that large areas of land in India have ambiguous ownership whereby the explicit (i.e. registered) owner of forest and pasture land has a number of more or less implicit joint owners.

... tenurial rights are defined not only by nominal ownership (registration in the land records) but by their products and use. As their usage changes, their predominant users may change, and even their nominal owners may change. Tenure is not a static characteristic of land: it is created, challenged or modified, and recreated. Tenure is a dynamic changing process with a number of societal actors and ultimately dependent on society for its acceptance. In this sense, all owners are tenants of society. Decision-making over various bundles of property rights are circum[scrib]ed by societal laws and regulations to varying degrees. Mutual expectations, shared normative ideals, and the degree of infraction and enforcement depends on society's enforcement of property right claims.

... The inescapable conclusion [is] that, to varying degrees, all land in India is in part common property. It is also partly State property, and it almost all has some private property rights. To address the common property problem in India, we must address the rights, obligations, and intentions of each of its joint-tenants. Obviously the most problematic lands are those which are registered under some kind of common ownership ... as they have the most overlapping rights and suffer the greatest ambiguity.

Source: Campbell, 1990

applied." What is important is to achieve a correct match between institutions and their physical, biological and cultural environments. This needs to be stressed, because some of the main initiatives in support of collective management of forests have attempted to apply uniform solutions to many different situations, with poor results. It has been argued, for instance, that this was one of the main reasons why the Social Forestry woodlot programme in India failed to become locally managed (Arnold and Stewart, 1991). Similar concerns have been expressed about its successor, the Joint Forest Management programme: "The proponents of JFM often appear blind to the social, ecological and political diversity of the nation, and apply the model irrespective of the location (although the consequences of the application are highly diverse)" (Hobley, 1996a).

Analysis therefore needs to be pursued within a framework that recognizes this diversity. It has been suggested that the main elements that should be addressed in any exercise for analysing and designing a common property regime for the management of local forests are:

- sources of incentives for individual behaviour;
- choices of strategies by individuals and resulting interactions among individuals and groups; and
- outcomes, in terms of forest resource and output sustainability, equity and efficiency of resource governance and management operations, etc. (Thomson and Freudenberger, 1997).

Common property management, or the lack of it, can usually be explained by interactions within this framework.

During the past decade, considerable progress has been made with the design of analytical models that help us understand what factors and interactions determine the circumstances under which common property management is likely to be appropriate and successful, and under which it is not (Bromley and Cernea, 1989; NAS, 1986; Oakerson, 1986; Ostrom, 1990; Wade, 1988). Key features that have emerged from these analytical models are summarized in Box 10. Common components among them include the following.

Components of the resource include:

- the size and boundary conditions of the resource;
- the ease with which it can be used by several or many users (subtractability), the ease with which those who are not members of the user group can be excluded (excludability), and its appropriateness for management communally rather than by individuals (indivisibility);
- the role of technology in its management and use, and the cost of alternative technologies; and
- the availability, structure and stability of markets for its outputs.

Components of decision-making arrangements include:

- mechanisms for collective and constitutional choice (i.e. procedures to set and change operational rules);
- operational rules (e.g. who has access, what actions must or may be taken or not taken, what information must be exchanged, what are the limits on user behaviour, what are the ways and means to obtain compliance, what are the jurisdictional boundaries); and
- roles of external legislation and regulations, and of enforcement and support bodies.

Components of operational features include:

- number of users and their legal positions;
- dependence of users on the resource;
- patterns of reciprocity and non-reciprocity;
- degree of homogeneity in assets, information, skills, cultures, values and payoffs; and
- efficiency and equity outcomes.

In the rest of this chapter, we draw on this framework to examine what lessons have been learned about management of forests as common property, using the historical and case material presented in earlier chapters. However, a number of qualifications need to be noted at this stage.

- To date it has not been possible to conduct rigorous analysis of the reasons for success and failure because of (a) difficulties in establishing indicators of determinants of organization; (b) the large number of dimensions and variables that need to be taken into account; and (c) the

Box 10: Factors Identified by Selected Authors as Affecting Local Organizations for Natural Resource Management

	Ostrom (1990, 1992)	*Wade (1998)*	*Oakerson (1986)*	*Bromley & Cernea (1989)*
Physical & technical characteristics of the resource system	Physical • Structure: Size Clarity of boundaries • Flow patterns: Predictability in time, across space & in quantity • Condition of the resource Technology • For withdrawing resources • For exclusion	Boundedness of resource Size Cost of exclusion technology	Capacity of the resource Excludability of the resource Subtractability/jointness Divisibility - physical boundaries	Nature of the resource
Characteristics of the group of users	Number of members Time horizon Proximity to resource & between users Extent of interaction - individualized or collective action Skills & assets of leaders Homogeneity vs heterogeneity of interests Norms of behaviour/culture Stability	Size of user group/number of members Boundaries of the group Location of resource & residence of users Users' knowledge Users' demand Power structure Mutual obligations		Characteristics of the user of the resource
Institutional arrangements	Design principles • Member & access rules • Resource boundary rules • Appropriation (withdrawing) & provision rules • Collective choice arrangements • Monitoring & sanctioning rules • Recognition of rights to organize by external agents • "Nested enterprises" - multiple layers of nested enterprises Market conditions for the resource	Existing arrangements for discussion of resource problems Punishment rules Relationship between users & state - external rules & intervention	Decision-making arrangements: • Operational rules • Collective choice rules • External arrangements	Characteristics of the decision-making process • Type of resource regime - property rights • Legal, political environment
Relationships		Noticeability: ease of detection of rule-breaking free riders		Ecological stress: supply & demand conditions

Source: adapted from Rasmussen and Meinzen-Dick, 1995

difficulty of operationalizing many of the key concepts relating to the resource base, the users and the organizations themselves (Rasmussen and Meinzen-Dick, 1995).

- Much of the analysis of forest CPRs relates to the past, which may provide only a partial guide to the future. Studying surviving systems that are under stress or in decline may yield only limited information about which conditions favour successful introduction of new and contemporary forms of common property management.

- Most past study of common property management was based not on forest-based resources but on fisheries, irrigation and range management. As was noted earlier, forest products users often have the option of meeting at least part of their needs from other sources if their forest CPRs become depleted. In contrast, users of many fish, water and range resources are unlikely to have such a choice. Their incentives to secure collective management are therefore likely to be more compelling than those of forest products users, and success with an approach to management of CPRs in these sectors will not necessarily be relevant to the forest-based sector.

- Finally, several recent intervention programmes, such as the Social Forestry programmes in India, have been concerned not with the appropriation of flows of outputs from an existing resource, but with creation of a new and different resource. This is likely to present quite a different set of governance problems (Gardner *et al.,* 1990). Analysis of the effectiveness of one may therefore be of limited relevance to understanding the other.

The following sections focus on four dimensions of experience of particular concern to common property management: (1) the attributes of the resource, the user community and the local institutional mechanisms through which the community manages its resources; (2) the impact of commercialization, and other economic opportunities and pressures, on common property management; (3) the vulnerability of common property systems to conflict and dispute and how this relates to the legal framework of common property; and (4) ways in which the state supports or otherwise intervenes in common property systems.

Identifying Local Circumstances Favourable to Common Property Management

By definition, collective systems can function only if the group is organized or can organize itself to function collectively. A degree of coordination between users is necessary in order to create and enforce rules of use and to provide individual members with access to inputs and services that are more effective when organized collectively. The literature on the subject suggests a number of factors that might affect the capacity of local institutions to organize the management of forests as common property (see Box 11). The discussion that follows concentrates on three key areas (Rasmussen and Meinzen-Dick, 1995):

- physical and technical characteristics of the resource;
- characteristics of the group of users; and
- attributes of institutional arrangements.

Box 11: Factors Affecting Cooperation in Local Organizations for Natural Resource Management[1]

- Relative benefits of cooperation (over alternatives)
- Size of the user group
- Users' perceptions of time horizon
- Degree of communication between players
- Expectations
- Degree of trust
- Willingness to try cooperation
- Catalysts to initiate cooperation
- Stability of the group
- Existence of other cooperative structures
- Non-anonymous relationship between members
- Content of social norms

1 Identified as affecting the degree or possibility of cooperation from discussion in the literature of the Chicken Game, the Assurance Game, Tit-for-tat Strategy, and the Fairness Game.

Source: Rasmussen and Meinzen-Dick, 1995

Physical and Technical Characteristics of the Resource

A basic characteristic is whether the resource has definable boundaries and can be protected. Management of a CPR is more likely to be effective if the resource is close to the user group and can be readily monitored. Another basic consideration is whether the resource can be divided up or not. An area of forest that can produce multiple products only as long as its multispecies structure is maintained more or less intact is more likely to induce collective management than tree stocks that could be split up into individually managed units, such as woodlots, or that generate outputs that can be produced from farm trees.

The incentive for users to invest in collective management is likely to be greater if the resource is capable of meeting a substantial part of users' needs, and if these benefits can be obtained rapidly and regularly. An early survey of indigenous user group systems in Nepal (Molnar, 1981) found that these were likely to be active only if the resource was sufficiently rich and substantial. If users felt their local resource was too poor or small to generate additional outputs commensurate with the efforts needed to protect and manage it, they were unlikely to make this investment. Within the CAMPFIRE programme in Zimbabwe, uptake was greatest in those communities where wildlife was an important part of their natural resource base.

By the same token, situations involving forest that is producing already are likely to provide a greater incentive to local collective management than woodlots that will produce only after several years. In West Bengal, the VPC programme has been more successful in areas well endowed with sal forest, which regenerates rapidly and produces early returns from non-timber products, than in those where returns had to be concentrated on plantations. In the Quintana Roo project in Mexico, interest has been greater in those ejidos where the forest is rich in mahogany and chicle than in those where returns from poorer forests compare less favourably with what can be earned from agriculture.

Therefore, the tendency to allocate degraded forest or scrubland for collective management in many programmes has probably often weakened the incentive for users to participate. The same is true if the resource allocated is too small to meet many of the users' needs. Resources that produce outputs that are valued locally, and products that members of the user group can benefit from in an equitable manner, are also likely to provide a stronger incentive to common property management than others that do not. The fact that these last two conditions were not met clearly became disincentives to local management in the Social Forestry woodlot programmes in India.

Another factor is the ease with which the resource can be managed by the user group. The Quintana Roo case, in which local communities are engaged in commercial logging and processing, shows that complex processes and sophisticated technologies can be handled at this level, given an appropriate institutional framework. In contrast, the fact that local communities were not trained and equipped to handle the tree management regimes they were expected to adopt has been cited as one reason why they were unwilling to take over responsibility for the Social Forestry woodlots in India.

Characteristics of the Group of Users

It has been widely argued that small homogeneous groups, confined to those with similar views on the use of the resource, are more likely to be successful than larger, more diverse groups. There are many instances where smaller groups do seem better able to sustain common property regimes, but the thesis that smallness is invariably desirable is being increasingly challenged. Although the task of dividing responsibilities and benefits may favour small and cohesive user groups, the task of managing and exercising control over the resource may call for a larger body that encompasses all those with a claim on the resource. Powers to negotiate with the state and to protect boundaries are also likely to favour larger bodies (Ascher, 1995; Stewart, 1991). For example, a recent study of the Van Panchayats in India has shown that larger groups are likely to have greater resources and therefore are better able to invest in protection and other services (Agrawal, 1996).

The benefits of size may also be achieved by 'nesting' the user group in a larger local body, such as the village leadership, a panchayat committee or the District Council. Alternatively, user groups can come together to form larger associations, as the VFAs in Korea did. Similarly, as was noted earlier, user groups in Nepal are getting together in order to share experience and obtain greater access to, and negotiating influence with, government services (Hobley, 1996b). On the other hand, it has been suggested that local institutions should be no larger than is necessary to include all those who need to have a voice in making decisions about the goods in question, the management system and the resources that need to be invested in that system (Thomson, 1992).

Though commonality of interest among users can have obvious benefits in terms of internal cohesion, the thesis that this should be sought invariably is also being questioned. It has been suggested, for instance, that heterogeneity can encourage the emergence of leadership and cooperation (Ostrom, 1990). However, being able to arrive at a consensus about who is to be included or excluded in a user group appears to be essential for its effective functioning.

Migration, mobility and market integration can all affect the stability of the community, and lack of stability can undermine the possibility of voluntary collaboration. Education or exposure to knowledge and ideas from elsewhere may alter members' perceptions of what they want from the CPR or from collective action. Changing attitudes and increasing wealth may introduce opportunities to benefit from privatization, or introduce the danger that the user group will become dominated or usurped by an emergent elite within the broader community. As communities change in these ways, the composition of a user group and its objectives are likely to need to change as well.

Attributes of Institutional Arrangements

Institutions are defined as the sets of rules by which societies live. They include formal rules established by law and official regulations, and informal rules established at the initiative of people and the groups that people form (see Box 12). Organizations are established to help (1) focus the development of rules; (2) formalize them through codification, legalization or social contract; and (3) enforce and implement them through incentives, persuasion or force (Gregersen *et al.*, 1993).

In some situations, a local institutional infrastructure capable of managing the available forest resources already exists in the form of traditional leadership, an elected local body or a user group dedicated to this task. More frequently, it takes the form of a local body with general responsibilities. However, its capacity to manage forests may be limited if, as is often the case, its boundaries and jurisdiction do not coincide with the boundaries of the forest to be managed, or if it has no relevant experience in collective management of other local activities.

The extent to which the interests of those who run or control the organization coincide with the interests of the forest user group, or groups, is also a substantial issue. The elected panchayat bodies in India and Nepal proved to be unsatis-

Box 12: Rules and the Creation of Rules

The role of rules

- Operational rules directly guide behaviour concerning a particular forest resource.
- Collective choice rules are rules for making operational rules (who can do so; under what conditions).
- Constitutional rules deteremine who is eligible to be included in the system, how collective choice rules can be made or changed, and who has the authority to create new units.
- Working rules guide people in making decisions, are understood by them, are monitored in application, and are enforceable; they may be formal or informal (written or unwritten).

Categories of rules

- Authorized relationships allocate rights, duties, liberties and exposures; they describe ability to control others and subjection to constraint by others.
- Authoritative relationships are the mechanisms by which rules are made, enforced, modified and superseded.
- Determining powers of officials are the authority that the latter have to make decisions without review or supervision by others (if these powers are considerable, authorized relationships and mechanisms can be manipulated significantly).

Source: based on Thomson, 1992, and Thomson and Freudenberger, 1997

Box 13: Guiding Principles for Effective Local Institutions for JFM in India

- **Viable social unit of organization:** Membership consisting of smaller, socio-economically and culturally homogeneous groups... tends to be a desirable, though not essential, condition... The majority of members should have a common interest around which to organize.
- **Organizational norms and procedures:** The local institution must evolve norms and procedures, whether formal or informal, acceptable to the majority of members for regulating their actions. These must be based on the principle of equitable rights and responsibilities of all members.
- **Accountability mechanisms:** For sustainability, each local institution must have effective mechanisms to ensure accountability of individual members and the leadership. These should ideally include: clear and accessible records, annual elections of representatives, participatory and open decision-making, power to recall corrupt representatives, penalties for violation of rules.
- **Conflict resolution mechanisms:** As periodic conflicts are inevitable, an effective local institution must have [access to] a variety of reliable conflict mechanisms. These could include: strong and trusted leadership, access to impartial and respected outside individual(s) or agencies, delegation of arbitration powers to the managing committee or other party.
- **Autonomous status:** For any local institution to genuinely function as the voice of its members, it must be an autonomous entity. For effective participation in a joint management agreement, its existence should not be controlled by the forest department; both partners may have equal right to terminate the agreement. The local institution should have independent legal status.

Source: Sarin, 1993

factory in this respect largely because of their predominantly political and bureaucratic agendas, and because they generally covered much larger areas and populations than the forest user group. Similarly, District Councils in Zimbabwe tended to put their interest in using the CAMPFIRE programme as a source of council income ahead of the claims on that income by the participating communities.

Another issue that has arisen widely is that an existing institution, reflecting social values from the earlier period when it came into existence, and long-standing and entrenched patron-client relationships within a community, may not adequately reflect the current interests and concerns of all its present members. In particular, there can be continued widespread exclusion of, or failure to properly involve, women and other disadvantaged groups (Hobley, 1996b; Sarin, 1993).

The need for concern about the equitable aspects of collective forestry initiatives can be considerable. As was pointed out earlier, in the review of programmes in India, interventions to increase the productivity of a CPR can change its use in ways that divert benefits from those who previously used it for low-value grazing, fuel, and other products and uses. The increase in the value of a CPR that results from bringing it into more productive use can itself create or heighten pressures to privatize it. There can therefore be losers as well as winners in the process of creating common property regimes.

Where suitable local institutions did not exist, programmes to encourage and support local management of forests have tried to create them, either building on what already exists or from scratch. The experiences reviewed in the last chapter illustrate some of the problems that can arise. The new institution may exclude some previous users of the CPR, or leave them worse off. For instance, by vesting authority in a local institution dominated by men, the position of women as users may become even weaker than before. Similarly, the claims of those adjacent to a forest may be given priority over those of users further away who are equally dependent upon it. Attempts to construct institutions to a particular formula can create groups that lack common interest or cohesion, precipitating conflict and dispute. The institution may simply not function effectively or may become dominated by particular interests or the forest department (Ascher, 1995).

A recent study on the subject (Thomson and Freudenberger, 1997) has consequently stressed the importance of carefully weighing the potentials for basing a common property management intervention on existing institutions, even with some of the limitations outlined above, against the difficulties of creating new institutions. Bruce (1996) has commented to the same effect: "One of the most difficult tasks in thinking through a [common property] system is whether one should rely upon existing institutions or try to create new institutions to manage the CPR."

Box 13 summarizes a set of guiding principles for effective local forest management institutions drawn up by an experienced observer of the programmes in India (Sarin, 1993). The following principles highlight a broader set of conclusions (McKean and Ostrom, 1995), which combine the lessons from long-enduring common property systems outlined in Box 5 with more recent experience.

- User groups need the right to organize their activities, or at least a guarantee of no interference.
- The boundaries of the resource must be clear.
- The criteria for membership in the group of eligible users of the resource must be clear.
- Users must have the rights to modify their use rules over time.
- Use rules must correspond to what the system can tolerate and should be environmentally conservative to allow a margin for error.
- Use rules need to be clear and easily enforceable.
- Infractions of use rules must be monitored and punished.
- Distribution of decision-making rights and use rights to co-owners of the commons need not be egalitarian, but must be viewed as 'fair'.
- Inexpensive and rapid methods of resolving minor conflicts need to be devised.
- Institutions for managing very large systems need to be layered, with considerable authority devolved to small components.

A final point on this subject is to reiterate the need to match each institutional arrangement with the particular need in a given situation. Sometimes contracts can play an important role in securing agreement among the stakeholders involved in a particular situation, particularly where the broader legal basis for control and use is unclear or difficult to establish (Bruce, 1998). In some situations, more formal legal forms, such as registration as a non-profit corporation, may be necessary in order to secure an agreement (Lynch and Talbott, 1995). The Quintana Roo commercial logging and timber operation, with its supporting autonomous institution (the SPFEQR), and the joint safari operations with private enterprises of the CAMPFIRE programme, provide examples of other arrangements that have been found to be appropriate and effective in particular situations.

It is clear that in some situations it will be difficult to establish the conditions for effective local group management at all. When local institutions have broken down under market, demographic and political pressures, it is not to be expected that new local institutions capable of controlling resource allocation and use can be created easily. Under such circumstances, the low returns and high social cost associated with trying to control common resources may prove so unacceptable to users that they prefer to let the resource be exploited in an unregulated open access manner, or within rules laid down by the forest department or some other arm of government.

Economic Pressures and Opportunities

It is generally argued that, as households become more integrated into the market economy and seek to generate more income with which to purchase goods, the task of creating effective collective forest management systems tends to become more complex. Labour and capital are diverted from management to more remunerative activities, and the potential to sell forest products or use them in commercial activities increases the pressures to overharvest the forest resource. More complex controls are likely to be needed, and the diversion of output from local to commercial uses is likely to shift benefits away from those who had depended on the forest for essential supplies of fuel, fodder, etc., exacerbating the potential for dispute and conflict (Stewart, 1991).

Box 14: Commercialization Pressures on Common Property Systems

- Simple rules are unlikely to be workable if a commodity has high value. Incentives for appropriating the commodity and not cooperating are correspondingly high.
- Enforcement of rules is likely to be complicated by high value items, especially if the item is wanted by elites. Bribes and coercion to escape enforcement are more likely when high values bring in cash. Even outside observers can be bribed.
- Many organizations may not be flexible enough to adapt to rapid changes induced by commercialization. There may be no current rules on commercial products and there may be no past rules to learn from.
- High-value CPRs and commercialized products create incentives for outsiders and the state to appropriate the land and dispute legal claims.
- Legitimacy of CPR use is contested by regional, national or international organizations who see their interest at stake in use of a resource or commodity.

Source: McElwee, 1994

The viability of common property systems can be affected both indirectly, through changes in their broader economic settings, and directly, by market demand for products of the CPR itself. The Indian situation outlined in Boxes 4 and 5 illustrates some of the patterns of interaction at the level of the economic setting that can bear on common property management (Jodha, 1990). Access to markets enables people to purchase some of the goods they previously had to produce locally, encourages a shift within agriculture to cash crops and is likely to make agricultural opportunities and urban wage employment more rewarding than gathering activities. The exodus of labour to off-farm employment increases rural labour costs and discourages labour-intensive activities (which includes most activities based on forest product gathering and use) in favour of cultivated or purchased goods. Improved emergency relief programmes, combined with easier access to purchased supplies, are likely to reduce dependence on locally gathered forest products as a source of food, fodder, fuel, etc., in times of drought or other hardship.

With increasing integration into the market economy, the number of forest products used tends to decline and become increasingly concentrated (Homma, 1992; Wilkie and Godoy, 1996). In a recent study in an area in western Malaysia, for instance, it was found that the number of forest species used or sold as food, medicines, etc., had declined during living memory from 279 to 71 (Lim Hin Fui and Jamaluddin Ismail, 1994). Rising costs and market competition also tend to reduce the number of saleable forest products produced from forest sources, in favour of domesticated sources or synthetic alternatives. One consequence is a widely observed shift of production from CPRs and other natural forest sources to tree stocks maintained or established on farms (Arnold and Dewees, 1997).

In many situations, therefore, the incentives to engage in collective control and management of a local common pool forest resource can be weakened because of the reduced role of CPR products in local livelihood systems or the decline in the viability or competitiveness of activities based on CPR products relative to other activities.

When products of CPRs become commercialized and are subject to market as well as local demand, the collective management system comes under additional pressure. In a 1994 review of the subject, McElwee identified a number of factors that supported the view that commercialization has the potential to destabilize common property systems (see Box 14). The negative impacts of commercial pressure on a common property system are likely to include increasing pressures from users both inside and outside the user group, breakdown of the mechanisms for exclusion and control, and overharvesting and degradation of the resource. Other common consequences include increased social stratification within the group, with elites capturing the benefits (e.g. diverting supplies from subsistence use and users), which increases the likelihood of social conflict. In South America, where transactions have traditionally been based on reciprocity, exposure to market forces has led to even more fundamental breakdown within a community. The increased value commercialization gives to the resource is also likely to attract the interest of privatizers and encroachment (Runge, 1986). In addition, increased value may encourage the state to capture a share by charging royalties, establishing marketing boards or imposing restrictions that limit the ability of communities to compete with it as a producer. The consequence of all such pressures is likely to be increased transaction costs associated with maintaining a collective management system, often to the point where it is abandoned.

On the other hand, market demand can also give added value to CPR products, which could increase the economic incentive to control their use and management. McElwee (1994) identified the following factors that seemed to contribute to success in coping with commercialization of products of common property systems at the community level.

- There is a lack of colonial experience in the past.
- There is a history of involvement in commercial production within the community.
- There is strong group cohesion.
- Distribution of benefits is well defined (and so is not captured by elites or the state).
- The item has cultural significance in the community, which encourages cooperative harvesting or marketing (e.g. native crafts).
- Appropriate use rules exist or can be developed.
- Competition for the resource is limited, and has not been a problem in the past.

McElwee concludes from her review that "communities who seem best able to adapt to commercialisation are those with flexibility in determining whether to participate, which allows control over the degree of change, or those in which change has been less rapid."

Similar patterns can be found in common property systems still functioning in Europe. In the eastern Italian Alps, for instance, in areas where forests have been managed as CPRs for centuries, local institutions have adapted to shifts in management objectives from meeting local demands for fuel, etc., to organizing activities for producing and processing for the market, and most recently to generating economic benefits from tourism (Merlo, 1995; Morandini, 1996).

Some of the more successful cases identified in this study are those that needed, and were able, to create new institutional arrangements specifically geared to commercial operations. In Quintana Roo, the ejido groups function as industrial corporate entities, with the cooperative SPFEQR acting for all the groups in the market and in negotiations with the state. In Korea, it was again an umbrella cooperative organization, the NFFAU, that gave the village-level groups marketing strength and access to support services. In the CAMPFIRE programme, joint ventures with the private sector provided access to the specialized safari and hunting skills and experience of that sector. In the Van Panchayats in India, the management and marketing of the timber component of the resource is left to the forest department, with the communities getting a share of the proceeds.

Vulnerability to Conflict and the Regulatory Framework[14]

By its nature, common property use and management is vulnerable to conflict and dispute, because the creation of common property excludes users from outside the user group. The group's right to exclude is likely to be challenged by others who want access to the CPR. In addition, not everyone within the community is likely to agree with the creation of a common property regime for the resource: "We should expect the legal basis of common property to be challenged from both inside and outside the community" (Bruce, 1998).

Bruce (1998) distinguishes the following categories of dispute:

- disputes over exclusion, including
  - a) disputes over exclusion of former users under custom, and
  - b) disputes based on an asserted right by an outsider to use the resource under national law;
- disputes over collective choice processes;

14 This section draws in particular on Bruce, 1998.

- disputes over rules for resource management and enforcement of rules on members; and
- disputes with the state over its role.

It is argued that conflict is often a normal and even desirable element of social interaction, leading to needed changes (Pendzich *et al.*, 1994). However, disputes can debilitate and undermine the common property institutions involved, and if not resolved can lead to their eventual collapse (Bruce, 1998). Effective resolution of conflicts and disputes therefore becomes very important, but can prove problematic because of the exceptionally complex and confusing nature of the legal and regulatory context of common property.

The Legal and Tenurial Context

The understanding and resolution of many of the conflicts and disputes that arise over forest resources and uses usually is complicated by an overlapping and constantly changing tenurial situation. Indigenous tenure systems have different arrangements for land under different uses, with each tenure defined by the application to it of a specialized set of tenure rules. A tenure niche is defined in terms of who will use the resource and on what terms, with different community members having different rights within different niches. It is where niches overlap that conflict can occur (Bruce, 1998).

The extent of this complexity in the case of India is illustrated in Box 9. In their study of tenurial niches in Zimbabwe, Fortmann and Nhira (1992) stress the potential for conflict and dispute that overlapping niches create, and make the additional point that "tenurial niches must be recognized as evolving rather than static forms of social organization, even when their legal status remains static."

The situation usually is complicated further by the unsatisfactory nature of the broader legal framework. In most countries there is no single body of law dealing with common property. Instead, it is covered by parts of the laws concerning organizations, tenure and administration (Bruce, 1998). The legal basis for common property therefore is often very ambiguous and open to legal challenge.

The task of establishing the legal basis is made more difficult by overlapping and poorly reconciled systems of national and community land law and custom. In most countries, Western tenure and more recent systems designed to transfer control over land from local to the new political elites coexist with community systems, undermining the latter but seldom providing a satisfactory alternative because they are not enforced (see Box 15). This causes confusion, because the legal status of land and forest resources becomes unclear. Community-based rights can be challenged in terms of national law, and local groups can encounter difficulty in using the law to assert their rights (Seymour and Rutherford, 1990). Without secure legal backing, local people are also left in a weak position for negotiating change with government and can be left exposed to risk by even the best-intentioned initiatives introduced by the latter (Singh, 1986).

The examples of the Mexican ejido case, the Nepal case and, to some extent, the JFM case in India, show the benefits of having legislation specifically designed to support common property systems, i.e. legislation and regulations that provide authority both to communities and government agencies and enable them to generate the necessary rules, regulations and operational measures. However, governments are commonly slow to amend laws or pass new ones. The situation in

Box 15: Overlapping Modern and Customary Land Law and Custom

The typical outcome [of a country's history] is a legal layer cake. At the bottom are a variety of local, community-based systems whose formal validity may or may not be recognized by statutory law. Alongside them, usually quite limited in extent, are tenures from the colonial period, generally freehold (full private ownership) and leasehold. Over them are one or more layers of failed attempts to replace them with a unified national land law enacted after independence ... There is a major tension between these systems in the law and custom concerning land and natural resources.

Source: Bruce, 1998

Box 16: Processes Used in Conflict Resolution

CONCILIATION is an...	NEGOTIATION is a...	MEDIATION is the...
attempt by a neutral third party to communicate separately with disputing parties for the purpose of reducing tensions and agreeing on a process for resolving the dispute.	voluntary process in which parties meet face to face to reach a mutually acceptable resolution of the issue.	assistance of a neutral third party in a negotiation process. Mediators have no power to render a decision.

Source: Pendzich *et al.*, 1994

Thailand is not unusual; the government and government agencies have permitted an increasing measure of de facto local control and management and have drafted supporting legislation, but they have been reluctant to process it. The underlying uncertainty, and therefore the risk for local user and management groups, consequently remains.

Conflict Resolution The existence of a dual or multiple legal system means that people may have to face different fora in order to settle a dispute under the different legal systems. This complicates the task, at minimum causing lack of clarity and confusion to claimants. A recent study of disputes in forest use and management found that a substantial proportion of those involved in disputes or conflicts did not know what mechanisms existed to deal with their complaint, or what procedure to follow (Rose, 1994). These overlaps and this lack of clarity in the system favour the powerful, who can take advantage of the alternative opportunities the system provides (Bruce, 1998).

Since the bodies of legal rules may be unacceptable to those involved because of imprecision, lack of equity or lack of consistency with local practice, many disputes or conflicts may be addressed through means other than legal recourse. (Bruce, 1998; Rose, 1994). People may also be discouraged from using the legal system because of the cost, or because the courts are weak and are likely to be ignored. Alternative conflict and dispute management mechanisms employ collaborative approaches in order to reach mutually acceptable resolution of conflict through voluntary processes. The principal mechanisms are conciliation, negotiation and mediation (see Box 16). The form and source of intervention is likely to differ for different levels of dispute (Pendzich *et al.,* 1994). While a local arbitrator may be best for internal disputes, a neutrally aligned third party is likely to be needed for disputes between groups, and an impartial adjudicator for disputes with the state (Rose, 1994).

Such collaborative approaches need to be seen as a complement, as well as an alternative, to adversarial approaches or political action and can be particularly suited to many situations. It has been argued (Rose, 1994) that local institutions are probably best suited to settlement of disputes between members of the same user group. In contrast, government agencies or higher courts are likely to be better suited for settling disputes between user groups that do not share a local institution in common, that have not cooperated previously, or that will not accept local decisions. If the conditions under which the common property regime operates have been altered, groups in dispute are likely to need outside help in developing a conflict management system adapted to the new framework.

Bruce (1996) has noted that collaborative methods are the most frequently used approaches to conflict management in developing countries, but that once an adequate legal framework for forestry (see Box 17) is in place, adjudication has substantial advantages. These include the ability to compel participation and enforce a settlement over the objection of one or more of the parties.

The Presence of the State

For successful collective management, it is essential that the user group have security of access to and use of the resource. Effective local control, or joint control with the state, requires the willingness and ability of government to legitimize and empower the local institutions and help them enforce their rights.

As was discussed above, common property systems have long been subjected to pressures by governments wishing to increase their control over local activities and resources. This has accelerated recently as part of the process of nation-building in the postindependence period. The result has been "the ever increasing tendency of the state to expropriate the initiatives of the people" (Jodha, 1990). The inevitable resulting conflicts with existing power structures and allegiances encourage governments to take measures to undermine and remove previously functioning local governance and management systems, and replace them with political and bureaucratic structures and regulations (Thomson and Freudenberger, 1997).

Decentralization and Devolution Concern with structural adjustment and reduction of the size and the role of government has recently seen the beginnings of a reversal of the accumulation of responsibility and power at the centre. This has led to moves to decentralize to the local level and to devolve to private and non-governmental sectors activities that they can handle as effectively and efficiently as the state. The increased interest in common property systems owes much to their relevance to these new priorities.

However, some of the consequences of the ways these new policies have been pursued can themselves threaten common property management. For instance, as was noted above, the widespread titling of land to individuals in many countries of Africa (on the advice of the World Bank and the IMF that this would encourage agricultural growth) threatens the complex of overlapping rights that previously enabled different categories of users to access some part of the resource on those lands (Neumann, 1996). Similarly, concerns have been expressed that the new law allowing Mexican ejidos to sell land, again undertaken in the name of increased agricultural efficiency, could undermine the present collective use and management of forest resources on that land (Goldring, 1995; Richards *et al.*, 1995).

Also, there are concerns about who benefits and who loses when governments decentralize

Box 17: Features that Need to be Included in National Law

- Constitutional protection for common property, comparable to other property rights, and care over regulation of trees and their use which undermine economic incentives provided by property to communities as well as individuals.

- The law on natural resource management, including the forestry law, should recognize generally or provide for recognition in particular cases of existing indigenous forms of common property, and organization for managing them. The provisions should be sufficiently flexible to allow modification of some elements of these forms by community by-laws. It should be possible to elect to use indigenous tenure rules about use, but to reform the organizations which manage the resource; or vice versa.

- There should be a co-management regime available, recognized both by the general law on natural resources and in the forestry law. It should allow shared management between a state agency and one or more local communities, and should be applicable in situations of a resource utilized by multiple communities, where it is not feasible for any one community to assume exclusive management. This regime should be available for both land that has been under community control and land that has been under state control.

- The forestry law should allow the state to delegate control over forest resources that have been under its control ... The law needs to allow for a contractual, negotiated process. Given the experience in these situations, it is likely that initial attempts to give communities access will be cautious. A minimum expectation as to delegation should be stated, but the framework should be relatively flexible and allow a good deal of fine tuning of forms to local circumstances. Community forestry provisions in forest laws can fill important gaps in general law, providing a fuller range of options for forests.

- Gender issues must be addressed, and are difficult whether one is dealing with indigenous or statutory institutions. Solutions include emphasis on membership organizations, with membership on an individual rather than a household basis; gender quotas on governing bodies; and initiatives limited to women (e.g. women's village forest management committees being contracted areas of forest).

Source: Bruce, 1998

responsibility for forest management to local levels. For example, the Social Forestry programmes in India were widely perceived as having adversely affected those who previously used the common lands on which the trees were planted for grazing, fodder, fuel and other produce – generally the landless and poorer members of a community (Arnold and Stewart, 1991).

A more widespread concern is the extent to which the state actually relinquishes power and responsibility through some of these programmes. One observer has pointed out:

> "Recent decentralisation activities within the forest sector in India could be considered to have led to greater penetration of the state into the village, without the villagers acquiring an equal degree of power to question the actions of the state. As the state continues to reassert effective ownership over forest land through forest management organizations, the presence of forest officials in these groups is considered to be an essential controlling feature. In many situations, village forest committees established under joint forest management have effectively become an arm of the Forest Department, rather than being developed as independent organizations that could challenge the authority of the department" (Hobley, 1996b).

The case material discussed above shows that this reluctance of the state to relinquish control is widespread, e.g. the delays in passing draft legislation in favour of community forestry in Thailand, the reluctance to use existing authority to empower indigenous forest protection committees if they are perceived to be too active in Orissa (India), the ineffectiveness of most of the measures in favour of indigenous groups in South America, and the devolution of authority in Zimbabwe to local government rather than to the user communities. Even in Nepal, with its unusually progressive policies and legislation, the state reserves the right to reverse the process of devolution of control over forest land to local groups, and retains ownership of that land.

Transition Issues within Forest Departments

Joint implementation of forest resource management systems with local groups confronts forest departments with tasks that are radically different from those conventionally associated with management of state forests for timber and watershed protection. Whereas the latter requires centralized bureaucratic structures and hierarchical decision-making, the former, involving provision of support to others to enable them to manage the forest resource, calls for a decentralized structure staffed to allow decision-making at the field level by those working directly with the user groups.

Recent studies have highlighted a number of problems that forest departments are likely to face in making this transition. It can be difficult for them to give up the power, status and control over budgetary and extrabudgetary resources and income stemming from their control over large areas of forest. Existing practices are usually well entrenched and strongly linked to the "patronage systems and rent seeking within government organizations and with outsiders [that] are often the real determinants of institutional behaviour" (Hobley, 1996b). The benefits of involvement in participatory forestry seldom appear to be as substantial or satisfactory.

The transition can be complicated by the fact that, in many countries, forest departments continue to be responsible for regulatory functions and direct management of large parts of the forest estate. Trying to combine this with transfer of control of parts of the forest estate to others creates understandable internal tensions and confusion. For instance, the following comment has been made in relation to Nepal: "A major problem is that the organization which has been given the responsibility for devolving control of forests to local communities also represents the interests of those who have most to gain by maintaining control of forests themselves. The Forest Department is being asked to use its authority to give away its authority!" (Gilmour and Fisher, 1991).

A second problem area relates to the contrast in approaches appropriate to the traditional and new tasks foresters face. Public forests are most effectively managed by development and application of management models and techniques that can be applied uniformly over large areas. This encourages risk-averse behaviour that conforms to the norms associated with these standardized tasks. This contrasts strongly with the diversity of physical and social situations that participatory forestry represents. These factors put a premium on innovation, responsiveness, willingness to take risks, learning from experience and flexibility, all attributes unlikely to be nurtured in the highly structured bureaucracy of the usual forest department (Hobley, 1996b).

It has also been argued that in some parts of the world the ability and willingness of forest departments to engage in participatory forestry is hampered by patron-client relationships that exist in public service organizations. Information is considered to be of value, to be exchanged for something of equal value, and therefore not to be made readily available to lower levels of the hierarchy. Such value systems inhibit the development of bottom-up planning (Hobley, 1996b).

The difficulties in moving toward decentralization have been aggravated in some countries by governments that set very ambitious targets for participatory forms of forestry. Understandable moves to introduce collective management as quickly and widely as possible have, on occasion, resulted in programmes on a scale so large that centralized control and uniform patterns of intervention are unavoidable.

Reports from common property programmes in South Asia have drawn attention to the particular difficulties that conflicting interests within forest departments cause for their field staff. They are caught between the need to conform to the values of their service and the necessity of being able to respond to the needs and aspirations of the communities that they are expected to assist. It has been found that at the early stage of participatory programmes, junior field staff can become severely overtaxed by the magnitude and unfamiliarity of the new tasks (Campbell and Denholm, 1993).

These difficulties encountered within forest departments help explain the reluctance by foresters to hand over responsibility for management. The result is that some programmes have been hampered by failure of forest departments to honour their new obligations or enforce the laws and regulations that enable newly empowered rightholders to secure their rights (Seymour and Rutherford, 1990; Thomson, 1992). Real progress is likely only when field staff feel involved and committed to the new approaches. Encouragingly, there are signs in countries where the transition is relatively far advanced, such as India and Nepal, that such a change in attitudes is beginning to happen.

NGOs as Intermediaries and Providers of Support Services

The rigidities and constraints faced by many forest departments in making the transition to a role that supports management of forests as common property have resulted in a situation in which NGOs occupy an important role in many collective forest management programmes. NGOs can play an intermediary role between state and users, can facilitate change at the village level and can act as trainers of government staff in community-organizing skills. In the Philippines and Thailand, and now in India, NGOs have constituted an important part of institutional support groups that have played a key role in identifying and negotiating mutually agreeable strategies. In the Philippines and India, lead NGOs are now producing guidelines and manuals that provide a framework for field worker activities. As noted above, specially created umbrella NGOs in Mexico and Korea play critical roles in linking producer groups to the market and support services.

Success depends on identifying the right NGO for the job. Not all NGOs are better equipped or skilled, or more appropriately motivated, than the government departments they seek to displace. Recently there has been increased awareness that some NGOs are pursuing their own agendas (e.g. related to environmental issues), which are not necessarily congruent with the interests of the populations they work with.

Another factor that can intrude is tension between NGOs and government or government departments, such as forestry departments, because of perceptions that NGOs are pursuing goals that conflict with the interests of government. It has also become evident that forest departments are sometimes delegating tasks to NGOs to avoid having to do them themselves, i.e. in order to "avoid internal change" (Dove, 1995). A better approach would make use of the complementary strengths of NGOs and forest departments, rather than treat them as alternative ways of providing external support to groups managing forests as common property.

Chapter 5: Conclusions

The management and use of forest resources and forest outputs seldom falls neatly into private, state or common property categories. Many, if not most, forests are characterized by multiple products and multiple users and are usually being managed in pursuit of multiple objectives. They therefore often exhibit a variety of overlapping tenure arrangements. There may be individual, corporate and collective rights to use of a resource that forms part of state property. Several different groups of users may have tenure rights to different products or to use at different times. Use may be managed or take place in an uncontrolled open access situation.

The balance and composition of the component regimes varies widely, both spatially and over time. Though many earlier collective regimes have declined or disappeared, in the face of demographic, social, economic and political change, many contemporary situations contain elements of common property. However, this still is often not recognized adequately, probably due to failure to understand the complexities of a particular tenure situation, or because these have been obscured by policies and practices biased towards privatization or control by the state.

This neglect is reflected in the relative paucity of information and analysis about the contemporary role of collective tenure relating to forest resources and outputs. Understanding is still imperfect, though it is improving rapidly. As is evident in this study, some lessons of experience are becoming clearer. The scope now exists for a more focused and effective application of what is now known to the design and implementation of interventions in many situations. It is also possible to identify areas where additional study is needed. This final chapter focuses on three dimensions of the subject that need to be addressed in application, through research and at the policy level:

- the framework of broader factors that determine whether collective management is likely to be appropriate and feasible;
- key issues that governments and government services will have to address in order to support local management of forests as common property; and
- the interplay among local factors that affect the capacity and motivation of groups of users to organize the management of use of a resource.

Broader Factors Affecting Choice of Forest Management Regimes

Because management of forests as common property is by definition situation-specific (i.e. tied to particular local user groups or communities) most attention has been focused on the microfactors that bear on its functioning at this level. Investigation and intervention have mainly been concerned with interrelationships between the resource, the community and its institutions, and other features of the local situation. However, the success of local solutions is ultimately governed by broader political, economic and institutional factors that determine whether or not common property is an appropriate option. As has been discussed at some length above, the circumstances that previously favoured common property in the past have often been irreversibly altered by economic, demographic and social changes. If the influence of such changes is not understood and taken into account, there is a danger of putting into place interventions that try to sustain or create common property regimes and institutions that are not appropriate, or feasible, in a particular situation.

That this danger has not been avoided is evident in much of what has been proposed in support of a greater role for common property regimes. Thus, "the arguments for increased community control of common property too often call for the complete restructuring of society... or a wholesale change in the patterns of political life. Too often, they also invoke a romantic past and seek to reverse the economy to re-find self-contained subsistence systems. [But] the economic forces of modernization and commercialization, [which] are frequently anathema to traditional community based systems, cannot be wished away..." (Campbell, 1990).

The first stage in initiatives to introduce or to try to strengthen common property governance for forest resources and products therefore needs to include examination of the broader environment within which it would be expected to function. In doing so, a fundamental issue must be that of government's willingness and ability to provide an adequate legal basis for common property management. As has been shown throughout the study, policies, legislation and the ways in which these are applied and enforced widely discriminate against collective management of forests in situations where it would often otherwise appear to be appropriate. The potential to improve the prospects for sustainable management of forests as common property is therefore often likely to rest on whether governments are able to introduce and implement needed policy measures (Bruce, 1998).

It is necessary to distinguish between those policy changes that can be effected within the forest sector and those that depend on broader policy. The potential to introduce legislation to devolve responsibility for forest resources to the local level may prove to be limited if there are higher-level polices to extend control by central government. It is, therefore, important to be able to recognize the limits to how much change can be achieved within the framework of forest-oriented programmes. Equally, success is more likely if changes designed to strengthen local-level forest management and control can be shaped so that they are compatible with existing legislation and do not, instead, require new legislation.

Progress in identifying the circumstances under which common property systems are likely to be appropriate, and the national-level interventions are likely to be most effective, often requires further research into the interrelationships between local forest management and use practices and the surrounding framework of political, economic, social and demographic factors. Past research tends to have been narrowly focused on particular situations, products or species. Because the linkages among the various factors are usually complex and poorly documented, there are many dimensions that would benefit from investigation and analysis. However, the impact of market forces is central to many of the issues that arise, and it has been proposed that research centred on this topic could provide the best starting point (Ruiz Pérez and Arnold, 1996).

Supporting Local Collective Management of Forests

Strong promotion of communal management, often at the urging of donors, has frequently imposed pressures on forestry bureaucracies that they have often found difficult to absorb. The shifts in the demands put upon foresters have been profound, and criticisms that they have failed to respond appropriately have often aggravated their problems. Needs for change have sometimes been promoted ahead of the capacity to implement them. A period of consolidation could now be desirable, to allow more consideration of how best to address the difficulties that forest departments have encountered in adapting to management of forests as common property.

It is important to ensure that the institutional underpinnings of change are in place before initiating interventions. Though recognition of the importance of changes in attitudes and skills has led to a strong donor focus on training, this is unlikely to be productive unless it is preceded or accompanied by changes in the underlying culture and operating structures of forest departments (Hobley, 1996b).

Another important area that often needs to be addressed is that of achieving rapid progress in providing support and regulatory services over large areas without becoming centralized and dependent on standard approaches that cannot be adapted to the various types of situations encountered. Pilot projects that test and refine different approaches initially on a small scale constitute one well-tried approach. However, these have a higher cost in terms of the time and resources of the implementing agency, and it is necessary to develop strategies for moving from the pilot to the operational scale.

It may also be necessary to examine which state institutions are most likely to be effective in providing support to local collective management of forests. On occasion this may be more appropriately handled by an institution other than the forest department. A related issue is that of the role of NGOs, and the most appropriate balance between government and non-government institutions, in creating the support infrastructure for this area of forest governance and management.

More broadly, it may be necessary at this stage in many national programmes to critically examine the impact of shared and collective forest management initiatives by the state. Some observers have noticed a tendency to assess progress in terms of institutional change, or in terms of more effective and lower-cost protection of forests, rather than in terms of impacts on villagers' lives.

Local Factors Affecting Capacity to Organize and Manage

As shown in Chapter 4, in the section entitled "Identifying local circumstances favourable to common property management," analysis of experience has by now identified a number of factors that appear to be associated with successful local collective management of forest resources and products. To recapitulate, key factors include clear group membership criteria; the right to organize; the existence of a resource with definable boundaries; dependence on internal rather than external institutions; realistic internally set and monitored rules; and low-cost conflict resolution mechanisms (McKean and Ostrom, 1995; Rasmussen and Meinzen-Dick, 1995).

In a number of respects, the basic requisites for effective local institutions are therefore now clearer. Considerable experience of providing support to such local institutions has also accumulated (Thomson and Freudenberger, 1997). This has helped identify areas in which further research should refine understanding of the circumstances and institutional mechanisms appropriate to successful management of forest as common property. Issues that should benefit from further investigation include the following:

- Characteristics of the resource or output that facilitate collective control – For instance, recent analysis has suggested that it is easier to develop control and management systems for resources that generate stationary products (e.g. fuelwood) than for resources that produce mobile outputs (e.g. wildlife), and that ease of management is related to the cost and difficulty with which information needed for management decisions can be generated (e.g. data on potential sustainable yield) (Ostrom *et al.*, 1994).

- Measures to enable collective management regimes to deal with growing commercial demands – Such measures could include defining circumstances that would make it necessary to develop separate arrangements for managing the resource and its products, or would require creation of cooperatives or NGOs to provide technical and marketing services, or would make it necessary for the user group to register as a corporation.

- The impact of size and composition of user groups on their durability and effectiveness– Issues that need clarification include the circumstances under which the advantages of small group homogeneity are likely to be offset by the benefits that larger groups often enjoy; ways to maintain consensus and uniformity of purpose as groups become larger and more internally differentiated; and circumstances that favour collaboration among similar user groups, or their integration within larger 'nested' organizational structures, in order to achieve the advantages of larger size while maintaining the benefits of small size.

To sum up, with the first generation of government and donor programmes in support of collective forest management now well advanced in several countries, opportunities are emerging to take advantage of the experience that has accumulated, and the growing understanding of lessons that can be drawn from this experience, to target management of forests as common property more effectively. In doing so, it is important to recognize that some situations are further advanced than others in the process of building up or strengthening common property regimes. For some, the focus will have to be on exploring the potential for local collective management, identifying constraints and determining the scope for their removal. For others, the need will be to reinforce existing systems and ensure an enabling legislative environment and a forest department that can properly perform a supportive role. For those in areas where the process has reached the stage of largely self-sufficient local collective systems, the principal need is likely to be to ensure that they are not hampered in consolidating and improving on what has been achieved.

References

Agrawal, A. 1994. Rules, rule making, and rule breaking: examining the fit between rule systems and resource use. In E. Ostrom, R. Gardner & J. Walker, eds. *Rules, games, and common-pool resources,* pp. 267-282. Ann Arbor, University of Michigan Press.

Agrawal, A. 1996. *Group size and successful collective action: a case study of forest management institutions in the Indian Himalayas.* FTPP/IFRI Working Paper. Bloomington, IFRI Research Program Studies, Indiana University.

Amyot, J. 1988. *Forestland for the people: a forest village project in Northeast Thailand.* Community Forestry Case Study 2. Bangkok, FAO.

Anan Ganjanapan. 1995. *Will community forest law strengthen community forestry in Thailand?* Chiang Mai, Faculty of Social Sciences, Chiang Mai University.

Arnold, J.E.M. & Campbell, J.G. 1986. Collective management of hill forests in Nepal: the Community Forestry Development Project. In *Proceedings of the conference on common property resource management,* pp. 425-454. Washington, DC, National Academy Press.

Arnold, J.E.M. & Dewees, P.A. eds. 1997. *Farms, trees and farmers: responses to agricultural intensification.* London, Earthscan Publications. [Also published as: Arnold, J.E.M. & Dewees, P.A. eds. 1995. *Tree management in farmer strategies: responses to agricultural intensification.* Oxford, Oxford University Press.]

Arnold, J.E.M. & Stewart, W.C. 1991. *Common property resource management in India.* Tropical Forestry Papers No. 24. Oxford, Oxford Forestry Institute.

Ascher, W. 1995. *Communities and sustainable forestry in developing countries.* San Francisco, Institute for Contemporary Studies Press.

Ballabh, V. & Singh, K. 1988. *Van (forest) Panchayats in Uttar Pradesh Hills: a critical analysis.* Research Note No. 2. Anand, Gujurat, Institute of Rural Management.

Berkes, F. 1993. *The interface between natural and social systems.* Background paper prepared for 'The Performance of Natural Resource Systems Workshop,' September 1993, Beijer International Institute of Ecological Economics, Stockholm, Sweden.

Berkes, F., Feeny, D., McCay, B.J. & Acheson, J.M. 1989. The benefits of the commons. *Nature,* 340 (6229): 91 93.

Birgegård, L-E. 1993. *Natural resource tenure: a review of issues and experiences with emphasis on Sub Saharan Africa.* Rural Development Studies No. 31. Uppsala, International Rural Development Centre, Swedish University of Agricultural Sciences.

Borlagdan, S.B. 1990. Community organizing in social forestry. In *Voices from the field: third annual social forestry writing workshop,* pp. 202-231. Environment and Policy Institute. Honolulu, East-West Center.

Bromley, D.W. & Cernea, M.M. 1989. *The management of common property natural resources: some conceptual and operational fallacies.* World Bank Discussion Papers No. 57. Washington., DC, World Bank.

Bruce, J.W. 1998. *Legal bases for the management of forest resources as common property.* Draft Community Forestry Note. Rome, FAO.

Campbell, J.G. 1990. *Whose land is this? Overlapping tenure, tenure transitions, tenure options and tenurial technology in India's common property resources.* Paper presented at the 'First Annual Meeting of the International Association for the Study of Common Property,' 27-30 September, Duke University, Durham, USA.

Campbell, J.G. & Bhattarai, T.N. 1983. *People and forests in hill Nepal: preliminary presentation of findings of community forestry household and ward leader survey*. Project Paper No. 10. NEP/80/30, HMG/UNDP/FAO Community Forestry Development and Training Project, Nepal.

Campbell, J.G. & Denholm, J. eds. 1993. *Inspirations in community forestry.* Report of the 'Seminar on Himalayan Community Forestry,' 1-4 June 1992, Kathmandu, Nepal. Kathmandu, ICIMOD.

Campbell, J.G., Shrestha, R.J. & Euphart, F. 1987. Socio-economic factors in traditional forest use and management. Preliminary results from a study of community forest management in Nepal. *Banko Janakari,* 1(4): 45-54.

Chambers, R., Saxena, N.C. & Shah, T. 1989. *To the hands of the poor: water and trees.* New Delhi, Oxford and IBH Publishing.

Chase Smith, R. 1995. *The gift that wounds: charity, the gift economy and social solidarity in indigenous Amazonia.* Paper presented at the 'Conference on Forest Ecosystems in the Americas: Community Management and Sustainability,' 3-4 February, University of Wisconsin-Madison, Madison, USA.

Chuntanaparb, L. *et al.* 1993. *Community allies: forest co-management in Thailand.* Southeast Asia Sustainable Forest Management Research Network Report No. 2. Berkeley, Center for Southeast Asia Studies, University of California.

Davis, S.H. & Wali, A. 1993. *Indigenous territories and tropical forest management in Latin America.* Environmental Assessments and Programs, Policy Research Working Papers Series 1100. Washington, DC, World Bank.

Department of Forests. 1996. Information from the community and private forest division database. Nepal, Department of Forests.

Dorner, P. & Thiesenhusen, W. 1992. *Land tenure and deforestation: interactions and environmental implications.* Discussion Paper No. 34. Geneva, UNRISD.

Dove, M.R. 1983. Theories of swidden agriculture, and the political economy of ignorance. *Agroforestry Systems,* 1(2): 85-99.

Dove, M.R. 1995. The theory of social forestry intervention: the state of the art in Asia. *Agroforestry Systems,* 30(3): 315-340.

Falconer, J. 1990. *The major significance of 'minor' forest products: the local use and value of forests in the West African humid forest zone.* Community Forestry Note 6. Rome, FAO.

Femconsult. 1995. *Study of the incentives for joint forest management.* Main report prepared for the World Bank, Washington.

Fisher, R.J. 1989. *Indigenous systems of common property forest management in Nepal.* Environment and Policy Institute, Working Paper No. 18. Honolulu, , East-West Center.

Forster, N. & Stansfield, D. 1993. *Tenure regimes and forest management: case studies in Latin America.* LTC Paper No. 147. Madison, Land Tenure Center, University of Wisconsin-Madison.

Fortmann, L. 1984. The tree tenure factor in agroforestry with particular reference to Africa. *Agroforestry Systems,* 2(4): 231-48.

Fortmann, L. & Nhira, C. 1992. *Local management of trees and woodland resources in Zimbabwe: a tenurial approach.* OFI Occasional Papers No. 43. Oxford, Oxford Forestry Institute.

Fox, J. ed. 1993. *Legal frameworks for forest management in Asia: case studies of community/state relations.* Program on Environment, Occasional Paper No. 16. Honolulu, East-West Center.

Fox, J. 1996. Opening statement on the paper on conflict and community forestry: legal issues and responses. Conflict Management Series. *Volume 3: Compilation of contributions made to the electronic conference on 'Addressing Natural Resource Conflicts through Community Forestry, January - May 1996'.* Rome, FAO.

Gardner, R., Ostrom, E. & Walker, J.E.M. 1990. The nature of common-pool resource problems. *Rationality and Society,* 2: 335-58.

Gasgonia, D.Z. 1991. Development assistance and property rights in the Philippine uplands: implementation priorities, integration, and coordination. In J. Fox, O. Lynch, M. Zimsky & E. Moore, eds. *Voices from the field: fourth annual social forestry writing workshop,* pp. 55-74. Environment and Policy Institute. Honolulu, East-West Center USA. [Revised version also in Fox, 1993].

Gibbs, C., Payuan, E. & del Castillo, R. 1990. The growth of the Philippine Social Forestry Program. In M. Poffenberger, ed. *Keepers of the forest: land management alternatives in Southeast Asia,* pp. 253-265. West Hartford, Kumarian Press.

Gilmour, D.A. & Fisher, R.J. 1991. *Villagers, forests and foresters: the philosophy, process and practice of community forestry in Nepal.* Kathmandu, Sahayogi Press.

Goldring, L. 1995. *State sponsored land certification and titling programs and changing state-producer relations: ejido reform in Mexico.* Common Property Resource Digest No. 33.

Gregersen, H.M. 1982. *Village forestry development in the Republic of Korea. A case study.* Rome, FAO.

Gregersen, H., Arnold, J.E.M., Lundgren, A., Contreras, A., de Montalembert, M.R. & Gow, D. 1993. *Assessing forestry project impacts: issues and strategies.* FAO Forestry Paper 114. Rome, FAO.

Guha, R. 1983. Forestry in British and post-British India: a historical analysis in two parts. *Economic and Political Weekly,* 18(45) / 18(46): 1882-1947.

Guha, R. 1985. Scientific forestry and social change in Uttarakhand. *Economic and Political Weekly,* 20(45) / 20(46) / 20(47): 1939-1950.

Hafner, J.A. & Apichatvullop, Y. 1990. Farming the forest: managing people and trees in reserved forests in Thailand. *Geoforum,* 21(3): 331-346.

Hardin, G. 1968. The tragedy of the commons. *Science,* 162(3859): 1243-1248.

Hobley, M. 1996(a). *Participatory forestry: the process of change in India and Nepal.* Rural Development Forestry Study Guide 3. London, Overseas Development Institute.

Hobley, M. 1996(b). *Institutional change within the forest sector: centralised decentralisation.* Working Paper 92. London, Overseas Development Institute.

Homma, A.K.O. 1992. The dynamics of extraction in Amazonia: a historical perspective. *Advances in Economic Botany,* 9: 23-31.

International Institute for Environment and Development (IIED). 1994. *Whose Eden? An overview of community approaches to wildlife management.* London, IIED.

Jodha, N.S. 1986. Common property resources and rural poor in dry regions of India. *Economic and Political Weekly,* 21(27): 1169-1181.

Jodha, N.S. 1990. Rural common property resources: contributions and crisis. *Economic and Political Weekly Quarterly Review of Agriculture,* 25(26): 65-78.

Kant, S., Singh, N.M. & Singh, K. K. 1991. *Community based forest management systems (case studies from Orissa).* Bhopal, ISO - Swedforest/SIDA/Indian Institute of Forest Management.

Kurup, V.S.P. ed. 1996. *New voices in Indian forestry.* New Delhi, Society for Promotion of Wastelands Development.

Lawry, S.W. 1989. *Tenure policy and natural resource management in Sahelian West Africa.* LTC Paper No. 130. Madison, Land Tenure Center, University of Wisconsin-Madison.

Lim Hin Fui & Jamaluddin Ismail 1994. *The uses of non-timber forest products in Pasoh Forest Reserve, Malaysia.* Research Pamphlet No. 113. Kuala Lampur, Forest Research Institute Malaysia.

Lindsay, J.M. 1994. *Law and community in the management of India's state forests.* Working Papers. Cambridge, Lincoln Institute of Land Policy.

Lynch, O.J. 1992. Securing community-based tenurial rights in the tropical forests of Asia: an overview of current and prospective strategies. *Issues in Development,* 11/92. Washington, DC, World Resources Institute.

Lynch, O.J. & Talbott, K. 1995. *Balancing acts: community-based forest management and national law in Asia and the Pacific.* Washington, DC, World Resources Institute.

Malhotra, K.C. & Poffenberger, M. eds. 1989. *Forest regeneration through community protection: the West Bengal experience.* New Delhi, Ford Foundation.

Malla, Y.M. 1994. *Sustainable use of communal forests in Nepal.* Paper prepared for the 'Workshop on Sustainable Use of Renewable Natural Resources,' 18-26 January, World Conservation Union, Buenos Aires, Argentina.

McElwee, P.D. 1994. *Common property and commercialisation: developing appropriate tools for analysis.* M.Sc Dissertation. Oxford, Oxford Forestry Institute.

McKean, M.A. 1986. Management of traditional common lands (Iriaichi) in Japan. In *Proceedings of the conference on common property resource management,* pp. 533-592. Washington, DC, National Academy Press.

McKean, M.A. 1995. *Common property: what is it, what is it good for, and what makes it work?* Paper presented at the 'International Conference on Chinese Rural Collectives and Voluntary Organizations: Between State Organization and Private Interest,' 9-13 January, Leiden University, Leiden, The Netherlands.

McKean, M.A. & Ostrom, E. 1995. Common property regimes in the forest: just a relic from the past? *Unasylva,* 46(180): 3-15.

Merlo, M. 1995. Common property forest management in northern Italy: a historical and socio-economic profile. *Unasylva,* 46(180): 58-63.

Messerschmidt, D.A. 1987. Conservation and society in Nepal: traditional forest management and innovative development. In P. Little & M. Horowitz, eds. *Lands at risk in the third world: local level perspectives,* pp. 373-398. Boulder, Westview Press.

Messerschmidt, D.A. ed. 1993. *Common forest resource management: annotated bibliography of Asia, Africa and Latin America.* Community Forestry Note 11. Rome, FAO.

Mol, P.W. & Wiersum, K.F. 1993. Asia. In D.A. Messerschmidt, ed. *Common forest resource management: annotated bibliography of Asia, Africa and Latin America,* pp. 24-97. Community Forestry Note 11. Rome, FAO.

Molnar, A. 1981. *The dynamics of traditional systems of forest management: implications for the 'Community Forestry Development and Training Project'.* Report to the World Bank.

Morandini, R. 1996. A modern forest-dependent community: the Magnifica Comunità di Fiemme in Italy. *Unasylva,* 47(186): 47-52.

Mortimore, M. 1996. *Land tenure and resource access in West Africa.* Paper prepared for 'Foncier Rurale, Ressources Renouvables et Developpement,' a joint programme under the Franco-British Initiative. London, ODI/IIED.

Murombedzi, J. 1992. *Decentralising common property resources management: a case study of the Nyaminyami District Council of Zimbabwe's Wildlife Management Programme.* IIED Dryland Network Programme Issues Paper No. 30. London, IIED.

Murphree, M.W. 1996. *Wildlife in sustainable development: approaches to community participation.* Paper presented to the 'ODA African Wildlife Policy Consultation,' 18-19 April, Sunningdale, U.K.

National Academy of Sciences (NAS). 1986. *Proceedings of the conference on common property resource management.* Washington, DC, National Academy Press.

Netting, R.M. 1981. *Balancing on an Alp: ecological change and continuity in a Swiss mountain community.* New York, Cambridge University Press.

Neumann, R.P. 1996. Forest product research in relation conservation policies in Africa. In M. Ruiz Pérez & J.E.M. Arnold, eds. *Current issues in non-timber forest products research,* pp. 161-176. Proceedings of the 'CIFOR Workshop on Research on Non-Timber Forest Products,' 28 August-2 September 1995, Hot Springs, Zimbabwe. Bogor, CIFOR.

Oakerson, R.J. 1986. A model for the analysis of common property problems. In *Proceedings of the conference on common property resource management,* pp. 13-30. Washington, DC, National Academy Press.

Oh, Ho-Sung. 1988. Economic development and changing forest problems and policies: the case of Korea. In Y.S. Rao, M.W. Hoskins, N.T. Vergara & C.P. Castro, eds. *Community forestry: lessons from case studies in Asia and the Pacific Region,* pp. 135-147. Bangkok, FAO and East-West Center.

Ostrom, E. 1990. *Governing the commons: the evolution of institutions for collective action.* Cambridge, Cambridge University Press.

Ostrom, E. 1992. Crafting institutions for self-governing irrigation systems. San Francisco, Institute for Contemporary Studies Press.

Ostrom, E. 1994. *Neither market nor state: governance of common pool resources in the twenty-first century.* IFPRI Lecture Series 2. Washington, DC, IFPRI.

Ostrom, E., Gardner, R. & Walker, J. 1994. *Rules, games, and common-pool resources.* Ann Arbor, University of Michigan Press.

Peluso, N.L. & Padoch, C. 1996. *Borneo in transition: people, forests, conservation, and development.* Singapore, Oxford University Press.

Peluso, N.L., Vandergeest, P. & Potter, L. 1995. Social aspects of forestry in Southeast Asia: a review of postwar trends in the scholarly literature. *Journal of Southeast Asian Studies,* 26(1): 196-218.

Pendzich, C., Thomas, G. & T. Wohigenant. 1994. *The role of alternative conflict management in community forestry.* Forests, Trees and People Working Paper 1. Rome, FAO.

Perl, M.A., Kiernan, M.J., McCaffrey, D., Buschbacher, R.J & Batmanian, J.G. 1991. *Views from the forest: natural forest management initiatives in Latin America.* Washington, DC, Tropical Forestry Program, World Wildlife Fund.

Plantilla, J.R. 1991. Community forest management: toward strengthening the Certificate of Community Forest Stewardship. In J. Fox, O. Lynch, M. Zimsky & E. Moore, eds. *Voices from the field: fourth annual social forestry writing workshop,* pp. 75-93. Environment and Policy Institute. Honolulu, East-West Center. [Revised version also in Fox 1993].

Poffenberger, M. ed. 1990. *Keepers of the forest: land management alternatives in Southeast Asia.* West Hartford, Kumarian Press.

Poffenberger, M. 1996. *Grassroots forest protection: Eastern Indian experiences.* Research Network Report Number 7. Asia Forest Network.

Poffenberger, M. & McGean, B. eds. 1996. *Village voices, forest choices: joint forest management in India.* New Delhi, Oxford University Press.

Poffenberger, M. & Singh, C. 1996. Communities and the state: reestablishing the balance in Indian forest policy. In M. Poffenberger & B. McGean, eds. *Village voices, forest choices: joint forest management in India,* 56-85. New Delhi, Oxford University Press.

Potisoontorn, M. 1990. Public land: a case study of Rajsamakki Forest Village, Soengsang District, Nakorn Ratchasima Province, Northeast Thailand. In *Voices from the field: third annual social forestry writing workshop,* pp. 103-116. Environment and Policy Institute. Honolulu, East-West Center.

Pragtong, K. 1988. Helping rural people help themselves: a report on Thailand's forest villages. In Y.S. Rao, M.W. Hoskins, N.T. Vergara & C.P. Castro, eds. *Community forestry: lessons from case studies in Asia and the Pacific Region,* pp. 205-219. Bangkok, FAO and East-West Center.

Pragtong, K. & Thomas, D.E. 1990. Evolving management systems in Thailand. In M. Poffenberger, ed. *Keepers of the forest: land management alternatives in Southeast Asia,* pp. 167-186. West Hartford, Kumarian Press.

Rasmussen, L.N. & Meinzen-Dick, R. 1995. *Local organizations for natural resource management: lessons from theoretical and empirical literature.* EPTD Discussion Paper No. 11. Washington, DC, IFPRI.

Richards, E.M. 1991. The forest ejidos of south-east Mexico: a case study of community based sustained yield management. *Commonwealth Forestry Review,* 70(4): 290-311

Richards, M. 1997. Common property resource institutions and forest management in Latin America. *Development and Change,* 28(1): 95-117.

Richards, M., Navarro, G. & Vargas, A.. 1995. *Decentralizing forest management and conservation in Central America.* Working Paper No. 93. London, Overseas Development Institute.

Rodriguez, S., Vargas, A., Dedina, S. & Stanfield, D. 1993. Latin America. In D.A. Messerschmidt, ed. *Common forest resource management: annotated bibliography of Asia, Africa and Latin America,* pp. 193-253. Community Forestry Note 11. Rome, FAO.

Rose, L.L. 1994. *Disputes in common property regimes (CPRs).* Madison, Land Tenure Center, University of Wisconsin-Madison.

Roy, S.B. 1991. Forest protection committees in West Bengal: emerging policy issues. In J. Fox, O. Lynch, M. Zimsky & E. Moore, eds. *Voices from the field: fourth annual social forestry writing workshop,* pp. 1-13. Environment and Policy Institute. Honolulu, East-West Center. [Revised version also in Fox 1993].

Rudel, T.K. 1995. When do property rights matter? Open access, informal social controls, and deforestation in the Ecuadorian Amazon. *Human Organization,* 54(2): 187-194.

Ruiz Pérez, M. & Arnold, J.E.M. eds. *Current issues in non-timber forest products research.* Proceedings of the 'CIFOR Workshop on Research on Non-Timber Forest Products,' 28 August-2 September 1995, Hot Springs, Zimbabwe. Bogor, CIFOR.

Runge C.F. 1986. Common property and collective action in economic development. In *Proceedings of the conference on common property resource management,* pp. 31-62. Washington, DC, National Academy Press.

Sabban, M.V.M. 1992. Managing decentralization in social forestry: a review of issues and strategies in the Philippines. In J. Fox, A. Flavelle & N. Podger. eds. *Voices from the field: fifth annual social forestry writing workshop*. Environment and Policy Institute. Honolulu, East-West Center.

Sarin, M. 1993. *From conflict to collaboration: local institutions in joint forest management.* Joint Forest Management Working Paper No. 14. New Delhi, SPWD and Ford Foundation.

Saxena, N. C. 1987. *Social forestry in the hill districts of Uttar Pradesh.* Kathmandu, ICIMOD.

Scoones, I. & Matose, F.. 1993. Local woodland management: realities at the grass roots. In *Living with trees: policies for forestry management in Zimbabwe.* World Bank Technical Paper No. 210. Washington, DC, World Bank.

Seymour, F.J. & Rutherford, D. 1990. Contractual agreements in Asian social forestry programs. Paper presented at the 'First Annual Meeting of the International Association for the Study of Common Property,' 27-30 September, Duke University, Durham, USA. [Revised version also in Fox 1993].

Shepherd, G. 1992. *Managing Africa's tropical dry forests: a review of indigenous methods*. Agricultural Occasional Paper 14. London, Overseas Development Institute. (Also in D.A. Messerschmidt, ed. *Common forest resource management: annotated bibliography of Asia, Africa and Latin America,* pp. 99-191. Community Forestry Note 11. Rome, FAO.)

Singh, C. 1986. *Common property and common poverty: India's forest, forest dwellers and the law.* New Delhi, Oxford University Press.

Snook, L.C. 1991. *Opportunities and constraints for sustainable tropical forestry: lessons from the Plan Piloto Forestal, Quintana Roo, Mexico.* Paper presented at the 'Humid Tropical Lowlands Conference: Development Strategies and Natural Resource Management,' 17-21 June, Panama City, Panama.

Society for Promotion of Wastelands Development (SPWD). 1992. *Joint forest management: concept and opportunities.* Proceedings of the National Workshop at Surajkund (India), August 1992. New Delhi, Society for Promotion of Wastelands Development.

Southgate, D. & Runge, C.F. 1990. *The institutional origins of deforestation in Latin America.* Paper prepared for the 'Conference on Economic Catalysts to Ecological Change,' February, University of Florida Center for Latin American Studies.

Stephen, L. 1991. Culture as a resource: four cases of self-managed indigenous craft production in Central America. *Economic Development and Cultural Change,* 40(1): 101-130.

Stewart, W. 1991. User groups and trees: a contractual approach. Unpublished draft manuscript.

Talbott, K. & Khadka, S. 1994. *Handing it over: an analysis of the legal and policy framework of community forestry in Nepal.* Cases in Development. Washington, DC, World Resources Institute.

Thomson, J.T. 1992. *A framework for analyzing institutional incentives in community forestry.* Community Forestry Note 10. Rome, FAO.

Thomson, J.T. & Coulibaly, C. 1995. Common property forest management systems in Mali: resistance and vitality under pressure. *Unasylva,* 46(180): 16-22.

Thomson, J. & Schoonmaker-Freudenberger, K. 1997. *Crafting institutional arrangements for community forestry.* Community Forestry Field Manual 7. Rome, FAO.

Tripathi, K.C. 1987. Local institutions involved in forest management: panchayat case studies. In R. Morse, C. Tingsabadh, N. Vergara, V. Vidyarthi, *et al.*, eds. *Peoples' institutions for forest and fuelwood development: a report on participatory fuelwood evaluations in India and Thailand,* pp. 107-136. Honolulu, East-West Center.

Vidyarthi, V. 1987. Participatory development issues and policy perspectives. In R. Morse, C. Tingsabadh, N. Vergara, V. Vidyarthi, *et al.*, eds. *Peoples' institutions for forest and fuelwood development: a report on participatory fuelwood evaluations in India and Thailand,* pp. 137-188. Honolulu, East-West Center.

Wade, R. 1988. *Village republics: conditions for collective action in South India.* New York, Cambridge University Press.

Wilkie, D.A. & Godoy, R.A. 1996. Trade, indigenous rain forest economies and biological diversity: model predictions and directions for research. In M. Ruiz Pérez & J.E.M. Arnold, eds. *Current issues in non-timber forest products research,* pp. 83-102. Proceedings of the 'CIFOR Workshop on Research on Non-Timber Forest Products,' 28 August-2 September 1995, Hot Springs, Zimbabwe. Bogor, CIFOR.

World Bank/USAID/GOI. 1988. National social forestry project: mid-term review. New Delhi, USAID.

Community Forestry Publications

Community Forestry Notes

1 Household food security and forestry: an analysis of socio-economic issues, 1989 (Ar/E/F/S)

2 Community forestry: participatory assessment, monitoring and evaluation, 1989 (E/F/S)

3 Community forestry: rapid appraisal, 1989 (E/F/S)

4 Community forestry: herders' decision-making in natural resources management in arid and semi-arid Africa, 1990 (E°/F)

5 Community forestry: rapid appraisal of tree and land tenure, 1989 (E/F/S)

6 The major significance of 'minor' forest products: the local use and value of forests in the West African humid forest zone, 1990 (E°)

7 Community forestry: ten years in review, 1991 (E/F/S°)

8 Shifting cultivators: local technical knowledge and natural resource management in the humid tropics, 1991 (E/F/S)

9 Socioeconomic attributes of trees and tree planting practices, 1991 (E/F**/S)

10 A framework for analyzing institutional incentives in community forestry, 1992 (E/F/S)

11 Common forest resource management: annotated bibliography of Asia, Africa and Latin America, 1993 (E/F**/S**)

12 Introducing community forestry: annotated listing of topics and readings, 1994 (E)

13 What about the wild animals? Wild animal species in community forestry in the tropics, 1995 (E)

14 Legal bases for the management of forests as common property, 1999 (E)

Community Forestry Field Manuals

1 Guidelines for planning, monitoring and evaluating cookstove programme, 1990 (E/F/S°)

2 The community's toolbox: the idea, methods and tools for participatory assessment, monitoring and evaluation in community forestry, 1990 (E/F/S)

3 Guidelines for integrating nutrition concerns into forestry projects, 1991 (E/F/S)

4 Tree and land tenure: rapid appraisal tools, 1994 (E/F/S)

5 Selecting tree species on the basis of community needs, 1995 (E/F**/S)

6 Marketing information systems for non-timber forest products, 1996 (E)

7 Crafting institutional arrangements for community forestry, 1997 (E)

Community Forestry Case Studies

1 Case studies of farm forestry and wasteland development in Gujarat, India, 1988 (E)

2 Forestland for the people. A forest village project in Northeast Thailand, 1988 (E)

3 Women's role in dynamic forest-based small scale enterprises. Case studies on uppage and lacquerware from India, 1991 (E°)

4 Case studies in forest-based small scale enterprises in Asia. Rattan, matchmaking and handicrafts, 1991 (E°)

5 Social and economic incentives for smallholder tree growing. A case study from Murang'a District, Kenya, 1993 (E)

6 Shifting cultivators of Indonesia: marauders or managers of the forest? Rice production and forest use among the Uma' Jalan of East Kalimantan, 1993 (E/Vietnamese)

7 Peasant participation in community reforestation. Four communities in the Department of Cuzco, Peru, 1993 (E)

8 The impact of social and environmental change on forest management. A case study from West Kalimantan, Indonesia, 1993 (E)

9 Tree and land tenure in the Eastern Terai, Nepal. A case study from the Siraha and Saptari Districts, Nepal, 1993 (E)

10 Tree and land tenure: using rapid appraisal to study natural resource management. A case study from Anivorano, Madagascar, 1995 (E)

11 Shifting cultivation in Bhutan: a gradual approach to modifying land use patterns. A case study from Pema Gatshel District, Bhutan, 1995 (E)

12 Farmer experimentation and innovation. A case study of knowledge generation processes in agroforestry systems in Rwanda, 1996 (E)

13 Developing participatory and integrated watershed management. A case study of the FAO/Italy Inter-regional Project for Participatory Upland Conservation and Development (PUCD), 1998 (E)

Community Forestry Working Papers

1 The role of alternative conflict management in community forestry, 1994 (E)

2 Participatory approaches to planning for community forestry, 1995 (E)

3 Forest resources and institutions, 1998 (E)

Community Forestry Conflict Management Series

- Proceedings: electronic conference on "addressing natural resource conflicts through community forestry," January-May 1996, (E)
- Integrating conflict management considerations into national policy frameworks. Proceedings of a satellite meeting to the XI World Forestry Congress, 10-13 October 1997, Antalya, Turkey, (E)

Community Forestry Guidelines

1 Women in community forestry: a field guide for project design and implementation, 1989 (E/F/S)

2 Integrating gender considerations into FAO forestry projects, 1994 (E/F**/S)

Community Forestry Audio Visuals and Slide Booklets

- Forestry and food security, 1993 (E/F/S)
- Fruits of our work: women in community forestry, Tanzania [slide booklet], 1991 (E)
- Gender analysis for forestry development planning - why? & how?, 1996 (E)
- Gender analysis for forestry development planning - why? & how? [slide booklet], 1997 (E)
- What is a tree?, 1994 (E/F)
- What is a tree? [slide booklet], 1995 (E)
- Women and community forestry in Sudan [slide booklet], 1991 (E)

Community Forestry Cartoon Booklets

1 Food for the future, 1990 (Bahasa/Burmese/Ch/E/F/Hindi/Lao/Malaysian/Portuguese/Sinhala/S/Vietnamese)

2 Our trees and forests, 1992 (Ch/E/F/S)

3 I am so hungry I could eat a tree, 1992 (Ch/E/F/S)

4 Fabulous forest factories, 1993 (Ch/E/F/S)

Other Community Forestry Publications

- Community forestry posters, 1997 (E)
- Forests, trees and food, 1992 (E/S)
- Forests, trees and people programme [brochure], 1998 (E/F/S)
- Forestry and food security [brochure], 1996 (E/F/S)
- Forestry and food security [poster], 1996 (E/F/S)
- The gender analysis and forestry training package, 1995 (E)
- The participatory process for supporting collaborative management of natural resources: an overview, 1999 (E)
- People and forests: community forestry at FAO, 1997 (E/F/S)
- Restoring the balance: women and forest resources, 1991 (E/F/S)

FAO Forestry Papers

7 Forestry for local community development, 1978 (Ar°/E/F/S)

64 Tree growing by rural people, 1985 (Ar/E/F/S°).

79 Small-scale forest-based processing enterprises, 1987 (E/F°/S°)

90 Forestry and food security, 1989 (Ar/E/F/S°) [Viet]

136 Managing forests as common property, 1998 (E)

E - English
F - French
S - Spanish
Ar - Arabic
Ch - Chinese
Viet - Vietnamese
** in preparation
° available electronically only

Our publications and videos are available from your regional focal point:

Anglophone Africa
FTPP/FAN
Forest Action Network
P.O. Box 21428
Nairobi, Kenya
Fax: (254-2) 718398
E-mail: fan@fanworld.org
Internet: http://www.ftpp.or.ke/

Central America
Facilitador subregional para Centroamérica
Apdo. Postal 8198 - 1000
San José, Costa Rica
Fax: (506) 280-2441
E-mail: cbrenes@sol.racsa.co.cr
Internet: http://polux.sdnp.org.pa/~rfc

Europe
The Editor, FTP Newsletter
Swedish University of Agricultural Sciences
Research Information Centre
P.O. Box 7034
S-75007 Uppsala, Sweden
Fax: (46-18) 671980
E-mail: daphne.thuvesson@kontakt.slu.se
Internet: http://www-trees.slu.se/

Francophone Africa
Facilitateur régional pour l'Afrique francophone
FTPP@IPD-AC
Institut Panafricain pour le Développement
B.P. 4078
Douala, Cameroun
Fax: (237) 403068
E-mail: ftppass@camnet.cm

Latin America and Caribbean (Spanish)
Revista Bosques, árboles y comunidades rurales
Av. Manuel Gómez 634
Apartado 11-0152
Lince, Lima, Perú
Fax: (51-1) 265-0441
E-mail: ftpp@sifocom.org.pe
Internet: http://www.cnr.org.pe/fao/index.htm

North America and Caribbean (English)
FTPP/NACARCE
North American & Caribbean Regional Center
5400 Grosvenor Lane
Bethesda, Maryland 20814, USA
Fax: (301) 897-3690
E-mail: istfiusf@igc.apc.org

South Asia:
FTPP Facilitator for South Asia
FTPP@WATCH
Women Acting Together for Change
P.O. Box 5723
Baneshor, Kathmandu, Nepal
Fax: (977-1) 473675
E-mail: watchftp@wlink.com.np
Internet: http://www-trees.slu.se/nepal/watchindex.htm

Southeast Asia
FTPP@RECOFTC
Regional Community Forestry Training Center
Kasetsart University
P.O. Box 1111
Bangkok 10903, Thailand
Fax: (66-2) 561-4880
E-mail: ftccor@nontri.ku.ac.th
Internet: http://www.recoftc.org/

Other regions
Community Forestry Unit
Forestry Policy and Planning Division
Forestry Department
Food and Agriculture Organization of the United Nations
Viale delle Terme di Caracalla
Rome 00100, Italy
Fax: (39-06) 5705-5514
E-mail: ftpp@fao.org
Internet: http://www.fao.org/forestry/FON/FONP/cfu/cfu-e.stm